The Development Trajecto
Eastern Societies

In the four volumes of *The Development Trajectory of Eastern Societies and the Theories and Practices of Socialism*, the author re-examines Marx and Engels' theories on the development trajectory of Eastern societies by integrating theoretical analysis of Marxist theories and a historical investigation of socialist revolution and socialist construction around the world.

Pointing out the guiding significance of five aspects of the basic principles of Marxism for studying how Eastern societies develop, this volume interrogates various assumptions that have prevailed in academia, addresses unexplained topics, and offers insight into the understanding of these basic principles. The result is a penetrating and specific understanding of Marxist basic principles and the development trajectory of Eastern societies.

Critical engagement with predominant understandings and a refreshing reformulation of Marxist theoretical bases make the book a key new reference for readers who are studying or are interested in Marxism, Marxist philosophy, and the history of philosophy.

Jiaxiang Zhao is Professor of Philosophy at Peking University, and has served as vice dean and director of the academic committee of the Department of Philosophy, as well as vice president and consultant of the Chinese Historical Materialism Association. His main research interests include Marxist philosophy and Marxist classic works.

China Perspectives

The *China Perspectives* series focuses on translating and publishing works by leading Chinese scholars, writing about both global topics and China-related themes. It covers Humanities & Social Sciences, Education, Media and Psychology, as well as many interdisciplinary themes.

This is the first time any of these books have been published in English for international readers. The series aims to put forward a Chinese perspective, give insights into cutting-edge academic thinking in China, and inspire researchers globally.

Titles in philosophy currently include:

Explanation, Laws, and Causation
Wang Wei

Secret Subversion I
Mou Zongsan, Kant, and Original Confucianism
Wenming Tang

Secret Subversion II
Mou Zongsan, Kant, and Original Confucianism
Wenming Tang

The Development Trajectory of Eastern Societies
Jiaxiang Zhao

Historical Evolution of the Eastern Mode of Production
Jiaxiang Zhao

Leaping Over the Caudine Forks of Capitalism
Jiaxiang Zhao

Theories and Practices of Scientific Socialism
Jiaxiang Zhao

The Principles of New Ethics
Volume 3: Normative Ethics II
Haiming Wang

For more information, please visit https://www.routledge.com/series/CPH

The Development Trajectory of Eastern Societies

Jiaxiang Zhao

Translated by Qin Li

Routledge
Taylor & Francis Group

LONDON AND NEW YORK

First published 2021 by Routledge

2 Park Square, Milton Park, Abingdon, Oxon OX14 4RN
605 Third Avenue, New York, NY 10017

Routledge is an imprint of the Taylor & Francis Group, an informa business

First issued in paperback 2022

Publisher's Note

The publisher has gone to great lengths to ensure the quality of this reprint but points out that some imperfections in the original copies may be apparent.

English version by permission of The Commercial Press.

British Library Cataloguing-in-Publication Data
A catalogue record for this book is available from the British Library

Library of Congress Cataloging-in-Publication Data
A catalog record has been requested for this book

ISBN: 978-1-138-33081-8 (hbk)
ISBN: 978-1-03-233604-6 (pbk)
DOI: 10.4324/9780429447600

Typeset in Times New Roman
by Deanta Global Publishing Services, Chennai, India

商務印書館
The Commercial Press

Contents

Preface

The historical materialism founded by Marx and Engels is the greatest achievement in the science of human thought. Their theory about the development trajectory of the Eastern society is a gem and occupies a pivotal position in the treasury of scientific thought. Without this theory, historical materialism would be incomplete and lackluster.

The proposition and contention of "the theory of Eastern society's development trajectory" encompass the logical sequence of three basic concepts: The East, the Eastern society, and the development trajectory of the Eastern society. Brief definitions of these concepts follow.

Conceptually, the East corresponds the West, each with its own bounds and scopes. Definitions of both require a coordinate system with their own axis. Historically, the coordinate systems of the East and the West have varied in their respective bounds and scopes. In ancient times, the Roman Empire, located in the West, was often regarded as the axis of the world's coordinate system due to the former's expansive territory and national power. With increasing East–West exchanges, the East, as perceived by the West, gradually extended in the direction of the rising sun, from west Asia and north Africa to south Asia, then to east Asia and finally to the entire non-Western world.[1] In recent human history, Western Europe, leading the world's economics, politics, and culture, has been regarded as the central axis of the world's coordinate system. To Western Europeans, anything beyond their own territory is the East, including Eastern Europe and Asia. More specifically, territory north and west of Caucasia of Russia is considered the Near East; territory east of the Caucasia and west and south of the Volga River, including today's Iran, Iraq, and Palestine, is considered the Middle East; territory east of the Volga River is considered the Far East. The Far East includes China, North Korea, Japan, and Siberia. No accurate definition of the "East" is found in the works of Marx and Engels. Their use and interpretation of the "East" largely agrees with the above understanding by the West.[2]

Conceptually, the "Eastern society" corresponds with the "Western society." In the era of Marx and Engels, Western European countries had entered capitalism through bourgeois revolutions and reforms while the countries beyond were still pre-capitalist. Western European countries were consequently labeled as the Western society. In contrast, pre-capitalist countries were called the Eastern society. The concepts of Eastern society and Western society, seemingly geo-graphical, are essentially historical. In his early 1850s article on India and China and his chapter "Pre-Capitalist Forms of Production" of the *1857–1858 Economic Manuscripts*, Marx explained how the pre-capitalist mode of production differs from the capitalist mode. (1) Laborers and their work conditions are directly cor-related. (2) Individuals are subjected to and cannot exist without a specific com-munity. (3) The economy is of a self-sufficient natural type, and labor production is for personal use rather than for commercial trade. (4) The country is divided into many isolated and self-sufficient rural communes combining agriculture and handicraft, which constitutes the basis of the Eastern autocracy. (5) There is no private ownership of land, a key to understanding the Eastern society.

"The development trajectory of Eastern society" conceptually parallels "the development trajectory of Western society." Marx and Engels believed that the Western society of their time was already a capitalist society, which would move toward a socialist society in due course through revolution or peaceful evolution. The pre-capitalist Eastern society has two development possibilities or prospects. One, after winning its socialist revolution, it directly enters socialism by leaping over capitalism. Two, it enters capitalism after disintegration of the pre-capitalist society and then moves onto socialism. The choice between the above two pros-pects depends on the prevailing international environment. As Marx and Engels' theory on the development trajectory of Eastern society focuses on how the Eastern society moves toward socialism, this book is accordingly titled *The Development Trajectory of Eastern Societies and the Theories and Practices of Socialism.*

The vast content of Marx and Engels' theory on the development trajectory of Eastern society comes down to two main points. The first addresses the "Asian mode of production" and its status in the sequence of social development. The second is about the trajectory of Russian social development: Whether Russian society or its rural communes could have directly entered socialism without the capitalist stage. Marx and Engels focused on the first point in their early and mid-dle years, and on the second in their late years.

From last two decades of the 1900s until now, Marx and Engels' theory of the development trajectory of Eastern society has seen a controversial debate in Chinese academia. Debaters include historians, philosophers, economists, politi-cians, and sociologists. The debate has generated both valuable insights into and misinterpretations of Marx and Engels. I write this book with the hope to clear misinterpretations and delve into the actuality of the theory of Marx and Engels on the development trajectory of Eastern society.

In the Preface of the third volume of *Capital*, in response to the distortion of Marx's theory of average profit rate law by some bourgeois economists at the time, Engels said: "A scientific investigator, when culling what is needed, should read original documents as intended by their authors, instead of reading into them what is not there."[3] In his correspondence of later years, such as *Engels to J. Bloch* (September 21–22, 1890), *Engels to Kautsky* (February 23, 1891), *Engels to Vladimir Shmuilov* (February 7, 1893), and *Engels to W. Borgius* (January 25, 1894), aiming at distortions of basic principles of historical materialism by young scholars like Bart, Engels reiterated the importance of studying historical materialism not through second-hand literature but through a Marxian lens based on Marx and Engels' original works such as *Theses on Feuerbach, The Eighteenth Brumaire of Louis Bonaparte, Capital, Anti-Dühring,* and *Ludwig Feuerbach and the End of Classical German Philosophy.*[4] We should regard these words of Engels as important guides for our study of Marxism and Marxian works, so as to avoid distortions of and deviations from Marxism, which would vitiate the essence of Marxism. The same attitude applies to the study of Marx and Engels' theory on the development trajectory of Eastern society.

Then, how do we derive accurate interpretations of the classics of Marx and Engels?

First, the interpretation needs to be based on history current at the authors' time, rather than on subsequent history or expediencies. For instance, Marx and Engels believed, up to their late years, that socialist revolutions would first succeed in developed capitalist countries. Although they held in their later years that Russian rural communes might realize socialism by leaping over the "Caudine Forks" of capitalism, but the prerequisite would be the proletarian victory in West Europe. However, the idea prevails in much Chinese academia that Marx and Engels, in their late years, believed that a socialist revolution may first happen and succeed in undeveloped Russia, which finds proof in the victories of the Russian October Revolution and of the Chinese Revolution. Such an idea interprets Marx and Engels based on history subsequent to their lives and thus may distort Marx and Engels by violating basic historicism.

Second, Marxist classics need to be read as a coherent organic whole, rather than as works of discrete historical periods. Scholars in China and beyond fabricate "two Marxes"—a young and an old Marx in opposition with each other. Such fabrication overlooks the organic coherence among Marxist classics. For instance, some scholars, without heeding related earlier works of Marx and Engels, only read their late works regarding the possibility of Russian rural communes to directly enter socialism by leaping over "the Caudine Forks" of capitalism. Consequently, these scholars believe that Marx held earlier that all countries and nations were destined for capitalism regardless of their specific conditions, and that Marx only later was of the opinion that some countries and nations might leap over the "Caudine Forks" of capitalism. In reality, the idea that a great number of countries and nations could leap over the Caudine Forks of capitalism already germinated in their early and middle-aged works (e.g., *The German Ideology, Principles of Communism, The Communist Manifesto,* and *Capital*). Their later proposition that Russian rural communes could realize socialism by leaping over the "Caudine Forks" of capitalism was not a momentary whim but reinforced continuity from earlier thoughts, only expressed more explicitly.

Third, we should read and understand the classics of Marxism as a process of dynamic development rather than as ossified immutabilities of fixed historical periods. Marxism is an ever-evolving theory. Statements by Marx and Engels about the same theoretical issues may change with historical conditions and their evolving personal understandings, as evidenced in their statements about the "Asiatic mode of production" and its role in historical progression. Misunderstanding and misinterpretation may easily arise if we fail to heed the evolution of and the inter-play among Marxist ideas of different times. To facilitate a clearer, more accurate, and less biased exploration of the concept of the "Asiatic mode of production" and its role in historical progression, this book is segmented into four periods: The pre-1853 period, the mid- and late 1850s, the period as represented by *Capital*, and the period after Morgan's publication of *Ancient Society*.

Fourth, we need to conduct comparative studies of canonical writings about Marxism, including both similarities and differences, both complementarity and contradictions among these writings. Otherwise, we may see only a dichotomy between Marx and Engels, as do some scholars. For instance, on the issue whether Russian communes can possibly leap over the "Caudine Forks" of capitalism, some Chinese theorists contend that Marx and Engels held conflictual views. Though it may seem that Marx supports while Engels denies such a possibility, it is essentially a misinterpretation. A careful comparative analysis of Marx and Engels may easily reveal that Engels not only validated but also predated Marx in proposing the idea of the "leaping over." It was in his 1877 *Letter to the Editorial Board of the Otechestvenniye Zapiski* that Marx first proposed the "leaping over" idea. In 1881, Marx further clarified this idea in *Letter to Vera Zasulich* and its drafts. However, Engels discussed the same idea as early as 1874 to 1875 when writing *On Social Relations in Russia*. In 1882, this issue was incisively explored in the *Preface to the Communist Manifesto (Russian Version, Second Edition)* co-signed by Marx and Engels. After Marx died, Engels did mention, in 1874 in *Notes on Social Relations in Russia*, the reduced and even lost possibility of Russian communes leaping over the "Caudine Forks" of capitalism. By then, the histori-cal conditions had changed. First, Russian populists and members of Narodnaya Volya failed in their attempt to overthrow the tsarist government, which remained the last reactionary fortress in Europe. Consequently, the possibility of a proletar-ian revolution in Western Europe by overthrowing the tsarist government was lost. Second, the rapid development of Russian capitalism and the further disintegra-tion of Russian rural communes had already made Russia a capitalist country, because of which there would be no leaping over of capitalism. Therefore, Marx and Engels complement rather than contradict each other on this issue.

Fifth, we must shun unilateral bias to fully understand classical Marxism. Classical Marxism represents a large body of comprehensive and balanced dis-cussions of a great variety of issues. However, some academics give inordinate and biased focus to particularities over holistic investigations—their narrowed focus on isolated trees causes them to lose sight of the forest. For example, in his *Capital* and its drafts, Marx explicitly criticized the ills and evils of capitalism and how it stymied productivity and social progress. However, he was also mindful of the tremendous role of capital in promoting productivity, civilization, and social progress. Some Chinese scholars only see Marx's criticism of the ills of capital-ism, while overlooking or even ignoring Marx's full recognition of the positive roles of capitalism. This book will demonstrate the great role of capital in promot-ing productivity, civilization, and social progress, from three aspects. First, capital promotes productivity and creates the material and technological conditions for future society. Second, it generates free time that propels the emergence of talents for future society. Third, it nurtures conditions for the birth of socialism. In short, this book will engage in a comprehensive exploration of the social role of capital.

Since China's policy of reforms and opening up to the world, many academic works in China have addressed Marx and Engels' theories of the development trajectory of the Eastern society. My book will not repeat what has been published but will focus on analyzing and clearing misinterpretations of Marx and Engels. I welcome my peer scholars' criticism of my views presented in this book.

This book is divided into four volumes. The first elaborates the theoretical basis for studying the development trajectory of the Eastern society, including different social forms and their classifications, the purpose of human activities and the regularity of social development, historical determinism and subjective choice and the interplay between the two, historical progress and its measurement, and the five basic principles integral to Marxism. Only when guided by the above principal issues of Marxism may we correctly interpret Marx and Engels' theory of the development trajectory of the Eastern society. The first part of the book discusses the above issues in a manner that differs from popular textbooks. Here are the specific differences. Instead of a linear presentation of Marxian principles, the author's discussion synthesizes existing scholarly views to derive unique insights, correct errors, and bridge gaps. The goal is to formulate fuller, deeper, and more specific discussions. For example, concerning "the purpose of human activities and the regularity of social development," most textbooks endorse "the congruence between the regularity and purposiveness of social development," while the author offers the revised view that "human activities are purposeful, and societal development is regulated by laws." As another example, concerning "social forms and their classifications," the author contends that the classifications of the five and of the three social forms are both Marxian propositions. They complement rather than oppose each other in their explanations of historical development. The author is critical of the view that dichotomizes the classifications of the five and of the three social forms or denies the latter. In addition, the author adds the concept of "technical social forms" in societal classification, a concept largely absent in most textbooks.

The second volume elaborates the concept of the "Asiatic mode of production" and its historical evolution. This part utilizes the framework of four historical periods, namely, the pre-1853 period, the mid- and late 1850s, the period represented by *Capital*, and the period after Morgan's publication of *Ancient Society*. This part is to demonstrate how much academic controversy is produced by inadequate understanding of the concept of the "Asiatic mode of production" and its role in historical progression. This part also compares the ancient societies of the East and of the West, to illustrate that ancient Greece and Rome typify the slave society while China typifies the feudal society of the longest and highest development. The feudal society of China, though rarely stagnant in its long history, gradually fell behind Western European societies since the late 16th century. This part also contends that the Germanic people's transition from the primitive

directly to the feudal society neither contradicts nor negates the Marxian classification of social forms. The historical limitations of Marx and Engels' views on
the Eastern society will be discussed as well. For example, the ideas that private
ownership of land does not exist in the East, and that the rural commune is the
basis of the Eastern autocracy are not in line with China's social and historical
reality. There is a great controversy over the "five golden flowers" in the study of
Chinese history, since the People's Republic of China. The "five golden flowers"
refer to: Stages of ancient Chinese history, the germination of Chinese capitalism,
the Chinese peasant war, feudal land ownership in China, and the formation of the
Han nationality.[5] The author's views on these issues will be presented in this part
of the book as well.

The third volume, titled *Reconsidering "leaping over the Caudine Forks" of
capitalism*, discusses the development trajectory of Russian society. Due to its
close connection with contemporary reality, this complex issue can be politically
sensitive. Since the 1980s, China's academia has paid much attention to and conducted heated debates over this issue. The debate largely concerns the following
questions. First, what kind of revolution is the "Russian Revolution" as discussed
by Marx and Engels? Second, regarding the development trajectory of Russian
society, did the young Marx contradict the old Marx? Third, over the same issue,
are Marx and Engels in contradiction? Fourth, did the victories of the Russian
October Revolution and of the Chinese Revolution prove Marx and Engels' theory of leaping over the "Caudine Forks" of capitalism? Fifth, is it a positive or
negative statement when Marx claimed that "the greatest strength of the general
philosophy of history is that it is suprahistorical"? Based on synthesis and criticism of existing academic views, this part of the book presents the author's views
on the above questions.

The fourth volume reflects on the socialist theory and practice. Marx and
Engels' theory on the development trajectory of the Eastern society focuses fundamentally on how it may realize socialism. The socialist practice of undeveloped
countries such as the Soviet Union and China follows, tests, and enriches the theory of Marx and Engels' scientific socialism. It confirms some while negates other
elements in the principles of socialism. Therefore, an investigation of these countries' socialist practice may play a significant role in the testing and expanding of
the theory of socialism. This part, the longest section that occupies one-third of
the book, includes eight segments: the evolution of the taxonomy of future societal forms in the works of Marx and Engels; a comprehensive discussion of the
role of capital; the future of socialism from a new perspective; Marx and Engels'
vision of the basic characteristics of future societies, the debate over whether a
single country can realize socialism in isolation; Deng Xiaoping's theory of the
preliminary stage of socialism; and Deng Xiaoping's contribution to the understanding of the essence of socialism, and to the theory of historicism. The theory
of scientific socialism of Marx and Engels is rich and profound. However, some
important concepts and principles of the theory have eluded general recognition,
resulting in a severe weakness in our study of the socialist theory. Those concepts
and principles include the historical evolution of the taxonomy of future societies

in Marx and Engels' works; the shift of perspectives in Marx, Engels, and Lenin's exploration of the destiny of socialism; Marx and Engels' understanding of factors within capitalism that may promote the spontaneous emergence of socialism; and whether one single country can realize socialism. Based on a systematic study of Marxist classics, this part presents the author's views on the above issues. Chronologically speaking, this part of the book encompasses these topics: Basic principles of the scientific socialism of Marx and Engels; Lenin's inheritance and development of the theory of scientific socialism under new historical conditions; Lenin's views on the characteristics of the economically and culturally backward countries' transition to socialism, and on methods of socialist construction; Deng Xiaoping's theory of the preliminary stage of socialism; and finally inheritance and development of the theory of socialism by China's theory of "socialism with Chinese characteristics." This part discusses both the basic principles of scientific socialism and its history as well as the interplay between the two.

The theoretical framework of this book combines theory and practice, particularity and generality, logic and history, and ideal and reality. Despite its focus on Marx and Engels' theory of the development trajectory of Eastern society, the book also discusses the principles and history of Marxism, combining historical materialism and scientific socialism.

Notes

1 Zhu Jianjin (1996). *Where Will the Eastern Societies Go – Marx's Theory of the Eastern Societies*. Shanghai, China: Shanghai Academy of Social Sciences Press. 4.
2 Yu Liangzao (2011). *Marxism's Orientalism*. Beijing, China: People's Publishing House. 69.
3 *An Anthology of Marx and Engels* (Vol. 7). (2009). Beijing, China: People's Publishing House, 26.
4 *Selected Works of Marx and Engels* (Vol. 4). (1995). Beijing, China: People's Publishing House, 668–669, 704–705, 721–722, 734.
5 Zhang Yue. The Achievements of "Five Golden Flowers" Can't Be Denied. *Chinese Social Sciences Today*. 2015-11-10.

Introduction

The basis of Marx and Engels' theory on the development trajectory of the Eastern society is a very complicated issue. This issue involves not only the identification of historical facts on the development of Eastern society, but also the understanding and application of basic concepts and principles of historical materialism. There are many differences and controversies between scholars in China and beyond.

It is very important to correctly understand Marx and Engels' theory on the development trajectory of the Eastern society to prevent misunderstanding and misinterpretation and to know well the correct theoretical basis. Part I mainly focuses on five aspects of the basic principles of historical materialism: Social forms and their classification; purposiveness of human activities and regularity of social development; historical determinism, subject choice, and their relations; historical progress and its measure; and the integrity of Marxism. These five basic principles of historical materialism have a direct guiding significance for studying Marx and Engels' theory on the development trajectory of the Eastern society.

1 Social forms and their classifications

The social forms and their classifications constitute one of the basic theories in historical materialism, and serve as a theoretical foundation for studying the development trajectory of the Eastern society. The most sensitive and controversial issues concerning Marx and Engels' theory of the development trajectory of the Eastern society are related to their theory of social forms and their classifications. Therefore, an accurate understanding of Marx and Engels' theory on the development trajectory of the Eastern society calls for an in-depth investigation of their views on social forms and their classifications.

Human society is a vast and complex system. Due to the interaction of various factors, social development often assumes varied stages and types. The concept of social forms concerns the structures and characteristics of different societal stages and types. According to the needs of social practices, we may classify societal stages and types using different angles and methods, mainly: the classification of the five social forms, the classification of the three social forms, and the classification of the technical social forms.

1.1 Classification of the five social forms

Based on production relations, Marx and Engels classified human history into five successive social forms: the primitive society, the slave society, the feudal society, the capitalist society, and the future communist society (with socialism as its initial stage). This classification takes world history as a whole. However, it does not mean that every country or nation must go through the succession of the above five social forms. Some Chinese scholars argue that Marx and Engels never proposed this classification; rather, it was Stalin who proposed it in *Dialectical and Historical Materialism* in 1938. Such argument contradicts historical facts. We can claim, rather accurately, that this classification exists in all representative works of Marx and Engels. To substantiate this claim, a chronological analysis is offered below of the works of Marx and Engels.

The German Ideology by Marx and Engels in 1845 to 1846 is the first book that marks the basic formation of the historical materialism. In this book, the two authors presented their initial classification of social forms and social development laws. They analyzed social structure and its evolution based on the contradictory movements of productive forces and production relations. They attributed human history to the development in production relations (forms of ownership) which in turn are attributed to productive forces. The embryo of their theory of social forms and social classification is based on different forms of ownership, which in turn are based on the development of productive forces and division of labor. They divided the pre-capitalistic history into three forms of ownership: the tribal ownership, the classical ancient communal ownership and state ownership, and the feudal or hierarchical ownership.[1] In terms of economic structure, the "tribal ownership" is equivalent to the public ownership of land by clan communes. In terms of social structure, the declining clan communes were replaced by the emerging slave society. Marx and Engels had not distinguished clan communes from rural communes at that time. The "tribal ownership" they referred to is equivalent to the ownership form in Western Europe when primitive societies transitioned into slave societies. However, without yet a scientific idea of the primitive society, Marx and Engels considered tribal ownership as the first independent stage in the development of human society. The aforementioned ancient communal and state ownership is generally equivalent to the slavery of ancient Greece and Rome. Feudal or hierarchical ownership refers to the feudal system in Western Europe. These three forms of ownership represent a chronological sequence rather than spatial juxtaposition. Marx and Engels believed that these three forms of ownership were the precursors to the capitalistic society. If we add the ownership forms of capitalism and communism (which will replace capitalism in the future), there are exactly five forms of ownership. Hence, we now have the classification of the five social forms: the tribal ownership society, the slave society, the feudalistic society, the capitalistic society, and the communistic society.

The Communist Manifesto, written by Marx and Engels between December 1847 and January 1848 and published in February 1848, describes the class structures and class struggles in the slave society, the feudalistic society, and the capitalistic society. It posits that the capitalistic society will be replaced by a future communist society. Marx and Engels believed that "the history of all hitherto existing society is the history of class struggles," as they had not yet found any classless societies. Engels' note to the above quotation seen in the English edition of *The Communist Manifesto* published in 1888 further explained this point:

In 1847, the pre-history of society, the social organization existing before recorded history, was all but unknown. Since then, Haxthausen discovered common ownership of land in Russia, Maurer proved it to be the social foundation from which all Teutonic races started in history, and by and by rural communes were found to be, or to have been, the primitive form of society everywhere from India to Ireland. Finally, Morgan made the brilliant discovery of the essence of the *gens* and its relation to the *tribe*, uncovering the prototypical inner organization of this primitive communistic society.[2]

The four social forms of the slave society, the feudalistic society, the capitalistic society, and the communistic society, together with the primitive society before the class society, constitute the five social forms under discussion.

Marx offered his first precise expression of his classification theory of social forms and their evolution in *Wage Labour and Capital*, published in April 1849. He said,

> *The relations of production in their totality constitute what is called the social relations, society,* and, moreover, a society at a definite stage of historical development, a society with distinctive characteristics. *Ancient* society, *feudalistic* society, *bourgeois (or capitalistic)* society are such totalities of relations of production, each denoting a particular stage of development in human history.[3]

Marx's three social forms of the classical ancient society, the feudalistic society, and the bourgeois society, plus the primitive communistic society (precursor to classical ancient society) and the future communistic society (to replace the bourgeois society), in that order, are the five social forms experienced or to be experienced in human history.

Marx made his first complete presentation of the evolutionary sequence of the five social forms in his *Preface to the Critique of Political Economy* written in 1859. He said, "In a broad outline, the Asiatic, ancient, feudal and modern bourgeois modes of production may be designated as epochs marking progress in the economic development of society."[4] Marx also pointed out that the capitalistic society will certainly be replaced by the communistic society, as dictated by the evolutionary sequence of the five social forms. Rather than spatially juxtaposed, different forms of the same society, the Asiatic, ancient, and feudal modes of production represent different epochs in human society. However, some theorists in China believe that what Marx called the Asiatic, the ancient Greek and Roman, and the feudal social forms are just three different modes of the same social form, which stands contrary to Marx's original intention. What follows is a discussion of the "Asiatic mode of production" and its role in human development.

A note by Marx for Volume I of *Capital* published in 1867 says:

> Small peasant economy and independent handicraft partially forms the basis for feudalistic production and partially coexists with capitalism after disintegration of the feudalistic production. At the same time, they form the economic foundation of the classical communities at their peak, after disappearance of the primitive oriental commune and before the slave society dominates production.[5]

This involves the social forms commonly known as the slave society, the feudalistic society, and the capitalistic society. The "primitive oriental common ownership" is equivalent to "the Asiatic mode of production" mentioned in the *Preface to the Critique of Political Economy.* Therefore, the evolutionary sequence of the five social forms is: the Asiatic society, the slave society, the feudalistic society, the capitalistic society, and the future communistic society that replaces the capitalistic society.

In *Anti-Duhring* written between September 1876 and July 1878, Engels regarded "slavery, serfdom or bondage, and wage-labour" as three successive social forms of a class society.[6] These, plus the pre-slave society and the future communistic society, give five social forms as well.

Morgan's *Ancient Society* published in 1877 played a significant role in completing Marx and Engels' theory of the five social forms. Before the release of *Ancient Society*, Marx and Engels learned that the Asiatic communes, the classical ancient communes, and the Germanic communes were not the most primitive forms. However, they had not yet developed knowledge on how these social forms emerged historically or what society was like before that. Therefore, in *Preface to the Critique of Political Economy* and *Capital*, Marx set the "Asiatic mode of production" as the first stage of human history. Morgan's *Ancient Society* used North American Indians' situation to demonstrate that patriarchal clans in Ancient Greece and Rome were derived from matriarchal clans. The Asiatic communes, the classical ancient communes, and the Germanic communes arose after the disintegration of their local patriarchal clans. In other words, these communes arose during the disintegration of their primitive precursors. By now, their positions in the development of human society were scientifically determined. The theory of the five social forms was finally complete when the primitive society, rather than the "Asiatic mode of production," was set as the first social form in human development.

In *Origin of Family, Private Property and the State* published in 1884, Engels stated:

> With slavery, which attained its fullest development under civilization, came the first great cleavage of society into an exploiting and an exploited class. This cleavage persisted during the whole civilized period. Slavery is the first form of exploitation, the form peculiar to the ancient world; it is succeeded by serfdom in the middle ages, and wage labor in the more recent period. These are the three great forms of servitude, characteristic of the three great epochs of civilization.[7]

Primitive society, the three class societies after the collapse of the primitive society, and the future classless communistic society give the evolutionary sequence of the five social forms.

Our brief review has now revealed that the theory of the five social forms was proposed by Marx and Engels in the 1840s and completed in the late 1870s and 1880s after arduous and profound theoretical exploration. This theory is visible throughout Marx and Engels' important and representative works. It's hard to conceive why some scholars would deny that Marx had once put forward the theory of the five social forms. What would be the basis of their denial? Negation of Marx's theory of the five social forms would require refutation of every single piece of evidence presented thus far, which would prove largely impossible. More than likely, few of the deniers of the theory of the five social forms have ever seriously investigated relevant works of Marx and Engels or whether the theory resonates with the actual course of world history. Some deny this theory, this work of a lifetime effort, perhaps merely on the basis of certain Western viewpoints, or their own preconceptions, or even personal preferences.

1.2 Classification of the three social forms

The classification of the three social forms was explicitly put forward by Marx in *Economic Manuscripts of 1857–1858*:

> Relations of personal dependence (entirely spontaneous at the outlet) are the first social form, in which human productive capacity develops only to a slight extent and at isolated points. Personal independence founded on objective dependence is the second great form, in which a system of general social metabolism, of universal relations, of all-round needs and universal capabilities, is formed for the first time. Free individuality, based on the universal development of individuals and on the subordination of their communal, social productivity as their social wealth, is the third stage. The second stage creates the conditions for the third.[8]

In this *Manuscript*, based on the development status of the human as a social subject, Marx classified human history into three social forms: the society of personal dependence, the society of objective dependence, and the society of the individual's all-round development. These three social forms are determined by the three macroeconomic operating patterns: natural economy, commodity economy, and product economy. Based on these three patterns, the three social forms of natural economy, commodity economy, and product economy, which appeared successively in human history, took shape. Accordingly, three social forms, as determined by the afore-mentioned three economies, emerged. An internal congruence exists between the three social forms and the three economies: the society of personal dependence is the society of natural economy, the society of objective dependence is the society of commodity economy, and the society of the individual's all-round development is the society of product economy. The "three social forms" are thus based on two paradigmatic sequences. A discussion of the characteristics of the society of personal dependence will be offered in the second part of the book. What follows is a discussion of the characteristics of the society of objective dependence and of the society of the individual's all-round development.

Characteristics of the society of objective dependence:

In a society of objective dependence, the human subject has no dominion over the object; the object dominates over the human subject. The interrelationship among objects exists as a force external to and controlling over the human subject. The object-to-object relationship camouflages the human-to-human relationship, particularly the relationship between the exploiting capitalist and the exploited worker. This constitutes the nature of the society of the objective dependence. More specifically:

First, in a society of objective dependence, the object created by the worker's labor is alienated from the worker. One's creation is divorced from one's living. This is because the products created by the workers (materialized labor) belong not to the workers but to the capitalists and become the latter's means to exploit and control the workers. As Marx said about the society of objective dependence, "The objective creation of one's labour acquires an increasing independence ... An increasing portion of social wealth becomes an alien and controlling force that stands against the labourer." Furthermore, the social wealth created by workers "belongs not to the workers, but to the personified conditions of production (i.e., capital), to the massive object of power, a power that subjects the laborer as its prerequisite and its opponent."[9]

Second, in a society of objective dependence, the social power of commodities and money becomes a power that is beyond and opposes the producer, alien to and divorced from and yet oppressive over the producer. All these results from the materialization of social relations are due to the division of labor and exchange. Marx points out,

> As the social character of production grows, so grows the power of money, i.e., the exchange relation establishes itself as a power external to and independent of the producers. What originally appeared as a means to promote production becomes a relation alien to the producers. As the producers become more dependent on exchange, exchange appears to become more independent of them, and the gap between the product as product and the product as exchange value appears to widen. Money does not create these antitheses and contradictions; it is, rather, the development of these contradictions and antitheses which creates the seemingly transcendental power of money.[10]

Third, in a society of objective dependence, although the production and exchange of each individual are conscious and purposeful, to the society as a whole, they are characterized by anarchy due to the two contradictions mentioned above. In the case of circulation, Marx says,

> Though the individual elements of this movement originate from the conscious will and particular purposes of individuals, nevertheless the totality of the process appears as an objective relationship arising spontaneously; a

relationship which results from the interaction of conscious individuals, but which is neither part of their consciousness nor as a whole subsumed under them. Their collisions give rise to an alien social power standing above them. Their own interaction appears as a process and compelling force which is independent of them.[11]

Fourth, in a society of objective dependence, due to the materialization of social relations amongst people, material production and social relations have become forces alien to and controlling over people. Conceptions that emerge therein become oppressive forces over people as well. As the conception is abstract, governance by the conception becomes "abstract governance." As Marx puts it, the objective dependence, as opposed to the personal dependence, is thus manifested: "The previously interdependent individuals are now ruled by abstractions. However, the abstraction or ideology is nothing more than theoretical reification of the controllers' material relations." As the rule via abstraction or via ideology facilitates and solidifies the power of the ruling class, "the belief in the eternity of these ideas, of these material states of dependence, is, of course, in every way confirmed, nourished and inculcated by the ruling classes."[12]

Fifth, in a society of objective dependence, science becomes an independent force that stands outside and opposite against the worker and in service of capital. The separation of laborers from the objective conditions of labor is a feature of the capitalist mode of production. In the capitalistic society, science has developed rapidly and has been widely used in production. Science is applied to the production process and materialized into production tools (machine or machine architecture). Eventually, science is fixed in the form of capital and becomes the means by which capitalists exploit workers economically and the force by which capitalists control the workers. Thus, science has become a means of separating, opposing, alienating, and governing workers. In this sense, Marx thinks that science has become an independent factor that is divorced from, opposes, and alienates the workers (laborers) in the production process. Science now resides in a domain outside the laborer and the objective conditions of labor.

Characteristics of the society of individuals' all-round development:

Marx and Engels stated in *The Communist Manifesto*: "In place of the old bourgeois society, with its classes and class antagonisms, we shall have an association, in which the free development of each is the condition for the free development of all."[13] In Marx's *Capital*, the society of individuals' all-round development is called a "community of free individuals," and the characteristics of it are summarized and explained. He states,

Let us now picture to ourselves, by way of change, a community of free individuals, carrying on their work with the means of production in common, in which the labour-power of all the different individuals is consciously applied as the combined labour-power of the community.

> The total product of our community is a social product. One portion serves as fresh means of production and remains social. But another portion is consumed by the members as means of subsistence ... Labour-time would, in that case, play a double part. Its allocation in accordance with a definite social plan maintains the proper proportion between the different kinds of work to be done and the various wants of the community. On the other hand, it also serves as a measure of the portion of the common labour borne by each individual, and of his share in the part of the total product destined for individual consumption. The social relations of the individual producers, with regard both to their labour and to its products, are in this case perfectly simple and intelligible, and that with regard not only to production but also to distribution.[14]

According to Marx's above discussion and other related expositions, the characteristics of a "community of free individuals" in a society of individuals' all-round development can be summarized as follows:

First, the means of production are owned by the public, i.e., jointly by all members of the society, therefore eliminating private ownership of the means of production and the exploitation by some of others.

Second, the conflict between private labor and social labor is eliminated. The total product of all individuals' labor in the community constitutes the social product, owned by all community members. The total product of the community is divided into two portions: one portion serves as fresh means of production and remains social. The other portion is consumed by the members as means of subsistence.

Third, personal consumer goods are distributed in manners determined by development stages. According to Marx's discussion in the *Critique of the Gotha Programme*, a society where individuals achieve well-rounded development can be divided into two phases. In the first, "from each according to his ability" and "to each according to his work" is the adopted manner of distribution. That is, personal consumer goods are distributed as assessed by the individual's labor-time contributed to the community. At the advanced stage, the manner of distribution is "from each according to his ability and to each according to his needs"; this made possible by abundant material wealth.

Fourth, the contradiction between use-value and value is eliminated. The purpose of production is for use-value instead of for value and surplus-value, thus eliminating the commodity market and the nexus between goods and currency.

Fifth, the society allocates labor-time in a planned manner, optimizes the apportionment between labor functions and personal needs, and abolishes the anarchy of social production.

Sixth, the divide between necessary labor and surplus labor, and the phenomenon wherein capitalists exploit the surplus labor of workers, are eliminated. The society becomes free of the gap between the increasing wealth of some and the increasing poverty of many. The process of production is liberated from poverty and antagonism.

Seventh, the conflict between free labor-time and surplus labor-time is eliminated, and the free development of each is prerequisite for that of all. Debunking the conflict between free labor-time and surplus labor-time in the capitalistic society, Marx says:

> The free time of the non-working parts of society is based on the surplus labour or overwork (the surplus labour time), of the working part. The free development of the former is based on the workers' expenditure of their entire time, enabling development only of the former. The development of some humans' capacities is premised on the deprivation of other humans' development. The whole of civilization and social development so far has been founded on this antagonism.[15]

In a society where individuals achieve well-rounded development, the basis of such antagonism is eliminated. Individual development would no longer hinder but conduce toward others' development.

Eighth, the measure of wealth is changed. In a society of objective dependence (i.e., a capitalistic society), labor-time serves as the yardstick for wealth. In a society where individuals achieve well-rounded development, the measure of wealth is no longer labor-time, but disposable time. Individuals' needs within the society will become the yardstick for necessary labor-time. The goal of production is prosperity for all. The social productive force will develop more rapidly, affording an increasing amount of disposable time and enabling everyone's free and full development. In Marx's words, "Free development of individualities becomes possible. Necessary labour-time is no longer maximized for production of surplus value. Instead, it is reduced to a minimum to enable every individual's free development in art and science."[16] In a society where individuals achieve well-rounded development, individuals will have gained freedom in material production due to the development of productive force and the increase in social wealth. Marx thus describes freedom in the field of material production,

> The socialized beings, a community of producers, rationally regulate their interchange with Nature, bringing it under their common control, instead of being controlled by Nature. With minimal expenditure of energy and with conditions most favourable to, and worthy of, their human nature, they interact with the material world.[17]

When an individual gains freedom in the realm of material production and all other social activities, s/he has made a leap from the realm of necessity to that of freedom.

1.3 Relationship between the "five social forms" and the "three social forms"

The theory of the "five social forms" and the theory of the "three social forms" are both different and internally unified. The differences between the two are manifested largely in the following aspects:

First, according to the theory of the "five social forms," human history is divided into five different social forms based on the nature of production relations. According to the theory of the "three social forms," human history is divided into three social forms based on the relationship between the laborer and objective conditions of labor. The society where the laborer and objective conditions of labor are inferiorly combined is the society of personal dependence or of natural economy; the society where these two are separated is the society of objective dependence or of commodity economy; and the society where these two are superiorly unified is the society of the individual's all-round development or of product economy. The relationship between the laborer and objective conditions of labor cannot be explained directly by the theory of the "five social forms."

Second, the theory of the "three social forms" illustrates the successive replacement of the three major social forms based on changes of the relationship between individuals and their communities. In the society of human dependence or society of natural economy, there are two communities. One is the primitive community, including clan communes, rural communes, and patriarchal families. The other is a community derived from the dissolution of the primitive community, such as handicraft guilds, commercial guilds, and various guild houses. Everyone lives in, is a member of, and is constrained by the community, and cannot survive upon leaving the community. In the society of objective dependence or of commodity economy, all the above-mentioned communities have disintegrated. Individuals are not dependent on a community and are no longer confined by a community. It seems that they have obtained freedom, which however is not real because they are relegated to a false community of classes and nations and ruled by this false community. In the society of the individual's all-round development or of product economy, a real community of "free individuals" has been established. In this community, everyone's development has become a condition for all people's development. Individuals gain true freedom and can fully develop their talents and capabilities. The relationship between individuals and their communities cannot be explained directly by the theory of the "five social forms."

Third, in the theory of the "three social forms," wealth is used as one basis for classifying different social forms, as already mentioned above and will not be repeated here. This is not covered in the theory of the "five social forms."

Fourth, the theory of the "three social forms" specifically focuses on investigation and analysis of the formation, characteristics, nature, and development laws of the society of objective dependence or of commodity economy, as well as the process that inevitably leads to the extinction thereof, revealing social relations covered up by the relationship between objects and the fetishism of commodity economy. In *Capital* and its drafts, Marx examined and analyzed the contradiction between private labor and social labor, between use value and exchange value of commodities, and between abstract labor and specific labor in the production of commodities, revealing the transformation of commodities into money and capital, and the intrinsic links in the transformation of surplus value into profit, the surplus value rate into profit rate, the profit into average profit, and the profit rate into average profit rate. By dividing profit into industrial profit, commercial profit, land rent, and interest, as well as through the triadic formulas of capital v. profit, land v. land rents, and labor v. wage, Marx revealed the deep people-to-people social production relations covered up by the superficial object-to-object and people-to-object relations in the capitalistic society, i.e., the relation between exploiting capitalists and exploited wage-workers, and the degree of exploitation therein. This profoundly explains the irrationality of the capitalist commodity economy and the cruelty of exploitation of workers, revealing objective dependence relations or the fetishism of the commodity economy, demonstrating that the inherent conflict in capitalism is bound to lead to its own disintegration and demise. This view finds no direct explanation in the theory of the "five social forms."

Fifth, in the theory of the "three social forms," different forms of extracting labor are used as the basis for distinguishing the three forms of civilization that emerged after the disintegration of the primitive community. These three forms of civilization include the slave society, the feudal society, and the capitalistic society. In Volume I of *Capital*, Marx says:

> The essential difference between the various economic forms of society, between, for instance, a society based on slave labour, and one based on wage labour, lies only in the mode in which this surplus-labour is in each case extracted from the actual producer, the labourer.[18]

In Volume III of *Capital*, Marx further stated:

> It is one of the civilizing sides of capital that it enforces this surplus labor in a manner and under conditions which promote the development of the productive forces, of social conditions, and the creation of the elements for a new higher formation better than did the preceding forms of slavery, serfdom, etc.[19]

This feature of the theory of the "three social forms" is not discernible in the theory of the "five social forms," which uses production relations to classify social forms.

The theory of the "three social forms" and the theory of the "five social forms," despite their contrasts, may not be juxtaposed in contradiction. Both proposed by Marx, the two theories complement rather than contradict each other in their explanation of the development of human history. The two theories are essentially consistent with each other, and the consistency is manifested largely in the following aspects:

First, all social forms, classified either into "three" or into "five," are economic in nature. The so-called economic social forms can be classified in terms either of productivity or of economy. In general, the term "social forms" means the same as "economic social forms," the former perhaps being an abbreviation of the latter. Since the 1980s, due to the emergence of technological social forms, people often use "economic social forms" as a concept corresponding to "technological social forms," as a way to differentiate between the two. Social

forms as classified by the theory of the "five social forms" are based on production relations, which are economic relations in nature; hence social forms so
classified are of course economic social forms. On the other hand, the theory of
the "three social forms" is based on the degree of human development, which is
determined by the operative macroeconomic patterns and relations between the
laborer and the objective conditions of labor. The operative macroeconomic patterns and the relations between the laborer and the objective conditions of labor
both are economic forms or relations. Hence, the social forms classified thereby
are economic in nature as well. Specifically, the social form in which the laborer
and the objective conditions of labor are unified is derived from ownership of
the means of production, the most important part in the relations of production.
Therefore, the classification of different social forms, based either on relations
between the laborer and the objective conditions of labor, or on production relations, is essentially the same.

Second, the theory of the "three social forms" and that of the "five social
forms" agree in their illustration of societal evolution from public ownership to
private ownership and then to a higher form of public ownership. The primitive community characterized by personal dependence in the theory of the "three
social forms" is a public ownership society, while the slave society and feudalistic society following the primitive community are private ownership societies;
the society of objective dependence or of commodity economy is also private
ownership society. The society of individual's all-round development is a public
ownership society, which is better developed. In the theory of the "five social
forms," the primitive society is a public ownership society; the slave society, the
feudalistic society, and the capitalistic society are private ownership societies;
and the communistic society (with socialism as its initial stage) is a public ownership society with greater development. The basic economic system in China's initial stage of socialism is one primarily of public ownership coexisting with other
forms of ownership. However, the future socialist society and the communist
society as posited by Marx and Engels are public ownership societies in which
the whole society shares the means of production. Our discussion here is of Marx
and Engels' classification of social forms, based on their conceptions about the
ownership forms of future socialist society and communist society.

Third, the theory of the "three social forms" and that of the "five social
forms" agree that human history evolves from a classless society to a class
society and then to a higher form of classless society. In the theory of the "three
social forms," the society of personal dependence or the primitive community of
natural economy is a classless society; the slave society (following disintegration of the primitive community) and the feudalistic society are class societies,
as is the society of objective dependence or of commodity economy; the society
of individual's all-round development (i.e., the product economy) is a classless society of higher development. In the theory of the "five social forms," the
primitive society is a classless society; the slave society, the feudalistic society, and the capitalistic society are class societies; and the communistic society
(with socialism as its initial stage) is a classless society of higher development.

It should be noted that in China's initial stage of socialism, class divisions still exist. The developed socialist society envisioned by Marx and Engels is a classless society. Our discussion here is of Marx and Engels' classification of social forms and thus will be based on their vision of the future socialist society and communist society.

Fourth, the theory of the "three social forms" somewhat introduces and summarizes the theory of the "five social forms." A deep analysis of the former will reveal the latter. The society of personal dependence or natural economy seen in the theory of the "three social forms" is based on the unification of laborer with the objective conditions of labor. This society can be divided into three development stages, which correspond with the primitive society, the slave society, and the feudalistic society as seen in the theory of the "five social forms." All members in the primitive society live in a community of clan, kin, tribe, or patriarchal families. The community belongings (or the objective conditions of labor) are shared among and united with members of the community. This seems easy to understand. However, it challenges our mind that the slave society and the feudalistic society are such a society as well. Marx seemed to have foreseen this challenge, and elucidated it in *Capital* and its manuscripts. He pointed out that slavery and serfdom still see no separation between the laborer and the objective conditions of labor,

> rather, one part of society is treated by the other merely as an inorganic and natural condition of its own reproduction. The slave stands in no relation whatsoever to the objective conditions of his labour; rather, labour itself, both in the form of the slave and in that of the serf, is classified as an inorganic condition of production along with other natural beings, such as cattle, as an accessory of the earth.[20]

To put it bluntly, in the slave and the feudalistic societies, slave owners and feudal lords (or serf owners) did not regard slaves and serfs as humans, but as the objective conditions of labor, not unlike livestock and lands. Therefore, they are one with the objective conditions of labor. Marx divided the society of personal dependence or of natural economy into three successive social forms—the primitive society, the slave society, and the feudalistic society. These three successive forms, plus the capitalistic society and the communistic society, give the historical sequence of five social forms. Therefore, the theory of "three social forms" is essentially congruent with the theory of the "five social forms."

These two theories, both proposed by Marx, complement rather than contradict each other. Both help explain historical development. Neither can replace the other. Some Chinese scholars promote one over the other. Others claim that Marx proposed only the theory of the "three social forms" or that Stalin proposed the theory of the "five social forms," which thus should be negated as Marxian. Reversely, some scholars contend that only the theory of the "five social forms" is scientific, while that of the "three social forms" is not and thus should be abandoned. Both above views are biased and one-sided.

1.4 Classification of the technological social forms

The "five social forms" and the "three social forms" are classified, directly or indirectly, on the basis of production relations, and thus are all economic in nature. In addition, we can classify social development stages or social types on the basis of productivity and technology, including technology-affected industrial structures. The social forms thus classified are called "technological social forms." The Stone Age, Bronze Age, Iron Age, Steam Age, Electrical Age, and Electronic Age, as humanity has experienced or is experiencing, in that order, represent the technological classification of social forms. The Stone Age was a time in which people lived on fishing and hunting and thus could alternatively be called "the fishing and hunting society." In the Bronze Age and the Iron Age, farming made great progress. Agriculture was the dominant industrial structure, and the societies in these eras can be called the "agricultural society." In the ages of steam and electricity, large-scale machine industry made great progress. The societies in these ages can be called "industrial society" where industrialization dominated. In the Electronic Age, information technologies and information industries become dominant in society, hence the name "information society." Thus, a technological classification of social forms, as formulated above, gives us the historical sequence of: fishing and hunting society—agricultural society—industrial society—information society.

The theory of technological social forms originated with Marx and Engels. In his 1859 *Preface to a Critique of Political Economy*, Marx discussed the concepts of "nomadic nationality," "fishing and hunting nationality," "agricultural nationality," and "commercial nationality," which in aggregate imply the technological classification of social forms.[21] In his *Economic Manuscripts of 1857–1858*, Marx quoted from James Steuart's *Inquiry into the Principles of Political Economy*, in his discussion of "non-industrial country." "Non-industrial country" is the stage of "non-industrial society" or "pre-industrial society." Quoting again from James Steuart, Marx also discussed "industrial society" and classified social forms into fishing and hunting society, agricultural society, and industrial society.[22] In a letter to Marx dated September 23, 1882, Engels said:

> By Bourgeois Society, we understand that phase of social development in which the Bourgeoisie, the Middle Class, the class of industrial and commercial Capitalists, is, socially and politically, the ruling class; which is now the case more or less in all the civilized countries of Europe and America. By the expressions: Bourgeois society, and industrial and commercial society, we therefore propose to designate the same stage of social development; the first expression referring, however, more to the fact of the middle class being the ruling class, in opposition either to the class whose rule it superseded (the feudal nobility), or to those classes which it succeeds in keeping under its social and political dominion (the proletariat or industrial working class, the rural population, etc., etc.) – while the designation of commercial and industrial society more particularly bear upon the mode of production and distribution characteristic of this phase of social history.[23]

The "Bourgeois Society" here is equivalent to the capitalistic society in economic social forms, while the "commercial and industrial society" approximates the industrial society in the classification of technological social forms. In his 1884 book *Origin of Family, Private Property and the State*, Engels introduced the American scholar Lewis Henry Morgan, who divided human history into three main eras (Savagery, Barbarism, and Civilization), and described the basic characteristics of each. Engels then concluded:

> The sketch which I have given here, following Morgan, of the development of mankind through savagery and barbarism to the beginnings of civilization, is already rich enough in new features; what is more, they cannot be disputed, since they are drawn directly from the process of production ... For the time being, Morgan's division may be summarized thus: Savagery – the period in which man's appropriation of products in their natural state predominates; the products of human art are chiefly instruments which assist this appropriation. Barbarism – the period during which man learns to breed domestic animals and to practice agriculture, and acquires methods of increasing the supply of natural products by human activities. Civilization – the period in which man learns a more advanced application of work to the products of nature, the period of industry proper and of art.[24]

Engels agreed with Morgan's division of history. What is presented here is essentially the classification of technological social forms.

Of the concept of "industrial society," Harvard professor Daniel Bell offers his explanation. He believes that Marx's theory of the mode of production was of two parts—the social relations of production and the forces or techniques of production (machinery). Bell said: "The theory of industrial society, which has been advanced most notably by Raymond Aron, takes off from the second of these two aspects of Marx's theory of the mode of production."[25] He added:

> If we restrict the term capitalist to social relations and industrial to techniques, then we can see, analytically, how the different sequences unfold. In this sense there can be socialist post-industrial societies as there could be capitalist, just as both the Soviet Union and the United States, though separated along the axis of property, are both industrial societies.[26]

Bell's "post-industrial society" refers to the commonly known information society. Two sequences of social forms appear here: one is of economic social forms based on relations of production (i.e., primitive society—slave society—feudalistic society—capitalistic society—communist society), and the other is of technological social forms based on productivity, technological development, and corresponding industrial structure (i.e., fishing and hunting society—agricultural society—industrial society—information society).

Despite its distant theoretical origins, the concept of "technological social forms" is rather new and not included in the original system of historical materialism. The addition of this concept into historical materialism is mandated by contemporary needs and realities and promises great theoretical and practical significance. Entering the 20th century, world history has witnessed two major changes, both elucidated by the theory of the interrelationship between the economic and the technological social forms.

The first major change started with the era ushered in by the October Socialist Revolution led by Vladimir Ilyich Lenin in 1917. Countries that were economically and culturally undeveloped entered socialism while advanced countries stayed stagnant in capitalism. This led to an incongruence between the economic and the technological forms of society. Although the disintegration of the Soviet Union and the upheavals in the Eastern Europe changed the international landscape, there can be no denying of socialism, seen in Russia's October Revolution, in the Soviet Union, in Eastern Europe, and in other socialist countries. Neither can we deny the tremendous impact the aforesaid events exerted upon world history.

Historical materialism contends that the forces of production determine the relations of production, and thus the technological social forms, as measured by forces of production and technological development and accordingly industrial structure, are the material and technical foundations for the economic social forms measured by the relations of production. This is the relationship between the economic and the technological forms of society. Take ancient Chinese history as an example. The Stone Age was a primitive society, the Bronze Age a slave society, and the Iron Age a feudalistic society. Classic Marxist writers have also offered their classification of social forms based on the interplay between economy and technology. Marx said in his book *The Poverty of Philosophy*, "The hand-mill gives you society with the feudal lord; the steam-mill, society with the industrial capitalist."[27] Lenin fully agreed with the description in the booklet *Basic Tasks of Soviet Electrification* by G.M. Krzhizhanovsky: "The steam age is the age of the bourgeoisie, and the electrical age is the age of socialism."[28]

Historical materialism believes that the decisive impact of productive forces on relations of production cannot be absolutized. Relations of production are constrained by many other social factors, not just by productive forces. Whether an existing relation of production will be replaced by a new one is ultimately determined by the level of productive forces. The same determination is also affected by the severity of conflict between forces of production and relations of production, between the economic foundation and the superstructure. In a class society, the determining factors may include class contradictions, class struggles, the configuration of forces among different classes, the current international environment, and the economic scalability defined by prevailing relations of production. The complex totality of the above factors may incur an incompatibility between the economic and the technological forms of society. This became particularly apparent when a succession of countries—backward in productivity, economy, and culture—embarked on the socialist road. Consequently, an intricate picture emerges in the contemporary world: countries of the same productivity and technological development (or of the same technological social forms)—such as the

Soviet Union and the United States; China and India—assume different relations of production and different economic forms. Reversely, countries of different productive forces and different technological developments (i.e., of different technological social forms) may share the same production relations or the same economic social forms. Take, for instance, capitalistic countries with a developed economy and those with an undeveloped economy. Countries with higher productivity and technological development (those of higher technological social forms) may be of lower economic social forms. In addition, due to unique social and historical conditions, countries with lower productivity and technology (those of lower technological social forms) may be of relatively higher economic social forms. For example, a contemporary gap exists between China on the one hand and, on the other hand, Western Europe, North America, and other developed countries such as Japan. In terms of productivity, China's GDP ranks second in the world. In terms of per capita income, however, China is still at the initial stage of socialism and lags far behind the above countries of advanced capitalism.

The second major change in world history, occurring in the 20th century, was the technological revolution led by microelectronics. In the 1950s and 1960s, the industrialization of capitalism came to an end, replaced by a new era variously known as "post-industrial society," "post-economic society," "post-civilized society," "post-bourgeois society," "super-industrial society," "technological electronics society," "programmed society," "affluent society," "new industrial society," "unified industrial society," "Internet society," and so on. From a broader perspective, the new technological society may be more accurately called "smart society," a concept that captures the characteristic intelligence of this new technological revolution. "Smart society" manifests itself in the fundamental change of "knowledge-intensive industry" replacing "labor-intensive industry." Knowledge and intellect have increasingly dominated the industrial structure, social production, and social life. "Smart society" may be divided into phases such as "information society," "biological society," and so on. Since the 1970s, information technology and information industries have become dominant in the industrial structure of economically developed countries. As such, these countries have officially entered the "information society." Information technology and information industries are also playing an increasing role in the industrial structure of China, now ranked as "intermediately developed." In this sense, China can be said to have *basically* entered the "information society." At the end of the 20th century, scholars in China and beyond believed that human history would enter the "biological society" in the 21st century. In my view, a country can be said to have entered the "biological society" when its biotechnology and bio-industries dominate the technological system and industrial structure. However, based on the current status of technological social forms, the economically developed and relatively developed countries are still in the stage of "information society."

The above discussions have clearly indicated that the classification and sequence of the technological social forms, with their theory deeply rooted in Marx and Engels, are truly reflective of the development of human history. The information society, as one development stage in technological social forms, witnesses the dominance of information technology and information industry in the technological systems and industrial structures of the society. Regardless of the development of human history and of modern science and technology, the time is ripe to enrich the theory of historical materialism with the concept and classification of the technological social forms. As early as 1985, in my thesis *Economic Social Forms and Technological Social Forms*,[29] I put forward the idea that the concept of technological social forms should be added into the theory of historical materialism. In 1987, I discussed the classification of technological social forms in my books *The Core of Historical Materialism and Contemporary Reality* and *New Technological Revolution and the Development of Historical Materialism*.[30] The same discussion is given in my textbooks *The Principles of Historical Materialism (new ed.)*, *A Course of Historical Materialism*, *Principles of Marxist Philosophy*, and *Introduction to the Basic Principles of Marxism*.[31] However, it's a pity that the concept and classification of technological social forms have not been included in most textbooks (not even in some recent authoritative ones) published in China concerning the discussion of the principles of Marxist philosophy and historical materialism. This indicates a clear gap in China between theoretical research and educational practice, the latter of which has not incorporated the forefront of research findings. In recent decades, the notions of "agricultural society," "industrial society," and "information society" have become well-known and are frequently used in China. However, they have not found their home in the Marxist theoretical framework. I hereby appeal again that textbooks on Marxist philosophy incorporate the concept and classification of technological social forms. This absence should not be allowed any further.

Notes

1 *An Anthology of Marx and Engels* (Vol. 1). (2009). Beijing, China: People's Publishing House, 521, 522.

2 *An Anthology of Marx and Engels* (Vol. 2). (2009). Beijing, China: People's Publishing House, 31. Emphasis added.

3 *An Anthology of Marx and Engels* (Vol. 1). (2009). Beijing, China: People's Publishing House, 724. Emphasis added.

4 *An Anthology of Marx and Engels* (Vol. 2). (2009). Beijing, China: People's Publishing House, 592.

5 *An Anthology of Marx and Engels* (Vol. 5). (2009). Beijing, China: People's Publishing House, 388.

6 *An Anthology of Marx and Engels* (Vol. 9). (2009). Beijing, China: People's Publishing House, 297.

7 *An Anthology of Marx and Engels* (Vol. 4). (2009). Beijing, China: People's Publishing House, 195.

8 *Collected Works of Marx and Engels* (Vol. 30). (1995). Beijing, China: People's Publishing House, 107–108.

9 *Collected Works of Marx and Engels* (Vol. 31). (1998). Beijing, China: People's Publishing House, 243–244.

10 *Collected Works of Marx and Engels* (Vol. 30). (1995). Beijing, China: People's Publishing House, 95–96.

11 *Collected Works of Marx and Engels* (Vol. 30). (1995). Beijing, China: People's Publishing House, 147–148.

12 *Collected Works of Marx and Engels* (Vol. 30). (1995). Beijing, China: People's Publishing House, 114.

13 *An Anthology of Marx and Engels* (Vol. 2). (2009). Beijing, China: People's Publishing House, 53.

14 *Collected Works of Marx and Engels* (Vol. 44). (2001). Beijing, China: People's Publishing House, 96–97.

15 *Collected Works of Marx and Engels* (Vol. 32). (1998). Beijing, China: People's Publishing House, 214.

16 *Collected Works of Marx and Engels* (Vol. 31). (1998). Beijing, China: People's Publishing House, 101.

17 *Collected Works of Marx and Engels* (Vol. 46). (2003). Beijing, China: People's Publishing House, 928–929.

18 *Collected Works of Marx and Engels* (Vol. 44). (2001). Beijing, China: People's Publishing House, 251.

19 *Collected Works of Marx and Engels* (Vol. 46). (2003). Beijing, China: People's Publishing House, 927–928.

20 *Collected Works of Marx and Engels* (Vol. 30). (1995). Beijing, China: People's Publishing House, 481.

21 *An Anthology of Marx and Engels* (Vol. 30). (2009). Beijing, China: People's Publishing House, 31–32.

22 *Collected Works of Marx and Engels* (Vol. 30). (1995). Beijing, China: People's Publishing House, 143.

23 *Collected Works of Marx and Engels* (Vol. 28). (1973). Beijing, China: People's Publishing House, 139–140.

24 *An Anthology of Marx and Engels* (Vol. 4). (2009). Beijing, China: People's Publishing House, 38.

25 Bell, D. (1984). *The Coming of Post-Industrial Society: A Venture in Social Forecasting* (Gao Xian, Trans.). Beijing, China: The Commercial Press, 51.

26 Bell, D. (1984). *The Coming of Post-Industrial Society: A Venture in Social Forecasting* (Gao Xian, Trans.). Beijing, China: The Commercial Press, 131.

27 *An Anthology of Marx and Engels* (Vol. 1). (2009). Beijing, China: People's Publishing House, 602.

28 *Collected Works of Lenin* (Vol. 38). (1986). Beijing, China: People's Publishing House, 117.

29 Zhao Jiaxiang. Economic Social Formation and Technological Social Formation. *Guangming Daily*. 1985-3-11.

30 Zhao Jiaxing. (1987). *The Core of Historical Materialism and Contemporary Reality*. Tianjin, China: Tianjin People's Publishing House, 396–404.

   Zhao Jiaxing & Liang Shufa. (1987). *New Technology Revolution and the Development of Historical Materialism*. Shijiazhuang, China: Hebei People's Publishing House, 62–96.

31 Zhao Jiaxiang et al. (Eds.). (1992). *The Principles of Historical Materialism*. Beijing, China: Peking University Press, 426–443.

   Zhao Jiaxiang et al. (Eds.). (1999). *A Course of Historical Materialism*. Beijing, China: Peking University Press, 450–457.

   Zhao Jiaxiang (Ed.). (1999). *Principles of Marxist Philosophy*. Beijing, China: Economic Science Press, 175–176.

   Wei Xinghua & Zhao Jiaxiang (Eds.). (2008). *Introduction to the Basic Principles of Marxism*. Beijing, China: Peking University Press, 148–149.

   Wei Xinghua & Zhao Jiaxiang (Eds.). (2015). *Introduction to the Basic Principles of Marxism*. Beijing, China: Peking University Press, 136.

2 The purposiveness of human activities and the regularity of social development

The relationship between the purposiveness of human activities and the regularity of social development is an important part of historical materialism. However, many ambiguities or even mistakes may challenge the understanding of this issue. As a result, it is necessary to clear these ambiguities and mistakes through accurate interpretation.

2.1 The proposition of "unity between the regularity and the purposiveness of social development" is unscientific

In *Ludwig Feuerbach and the End of Classical German Philosophy*, Engels says,

In one point, however, the history of the development of society proves to be essentially different from that of nature. In nature – in so far as we ignore man's reaction upon nature – there are only blind, unconscious agencies acting upon one another, out of whose interplay the general law comes into operation. Nothing of all that happens – whether in the innumerable apparent accidents observable upon the surface, or in the ultimate results which confirm the regularity inherent in these accidents – happens as a consciously desired aim. In the history of society, on the contrary, the actors are all endowed with consciousness, are men acting with deliberation or passion, working towards definite goals; nothing happens without a conscious purpose, without an intended aim. But this distinction, important as it is for historical investigation, particularly of single epochs and event, cannot alter the fact that the course of history is governed by inner general laws. For here, also, on the whole, in spite of the consciously desired aims of all individuals, accident apparently reigns on the surface. That which is willed happens but rarely; in the majority of instances the numerous desired ends cross and conflict with one another, or these ends themselves are from the outset incapable of realization, or the means of attaining them are insufficient, thus the conflicts of innumerable individual wills and individual actions in the domain of history produce a state of affairs entirely analogous to that prevailing in the realm of unconscious nature. The ends of the actions are intended, but the results which actually follow from these actions are not intended; or when they do seem to correspond to the end intended, they ultimately have consequences quite other than those intended. Historical events thus appear on the whole to be likewise governed by chance. But where on the surface accident holds sway, there actually it is always governed by inner, hidden laws, and it is only a matter of discovering these laws.[1]

As quoted above, Engels believes that human activities, though conscious and purposeful, may produce results independent of human will and purpose. Although the development of human history differs from that of the natural world, there still exists similarity between the two—both are ruled by objective laws that are independent of humans' will. The development of human history actually involves a natural historical course. Human activities are purposeful, whereas social development has its objective laws independent of human purpose. This may be a synopsis of the relationship between the purpose of human activities and the regularity of social development.

However, many Chinese theorists, for a long time, have not understood the relationship between human activities and social development as explained by Engels. The proposition of "the unity between the regularity and the purposiveness of social development" still prevails in current studies of historical materialism. This proposition is frequently used in the discussion of historical development. Both Marxists and non-Marxists use the proposition, which often appears in textbooks on historical materialism and Marxist principles. However, under scrutiny, the proposition proves to be historical idealism and is incompatible with historical materialism. Long prevalent in the history of philosophy, the proposition is often blindly used by scholars, including me, in their articles and textbooks on Marxist philosophy. For example, the title of Chapter 19 of *A Course in Historical Materialism*, for which I served as the chief editor, is no other than the "unity between the regularity and the purposiveness of social development." Therefore, for this misguided proposition and its negative impact, I'm not free of culpability. This unfortunate proposition in the study of historical materialism causes harmful effects and I should take certain responsibility. I am here to exonerate myself by deconstructing and de-problematizing the proposition.

I argued in *A Course in Historical Materialism* that "social forms are objective and material, and its development sees regularity; social laws are formed and enforced in human conscious and purposeful practices, therefore the development of social forms features purposiveness as well." Concerning the relationship between the regularity and the purposiveness in the development of social forms, we need to guard against two biases. One is undue emphasis on the objectiveness and regularity of social development but oversight of the subjectivity and purposiveness of it. Consequently, the historical materialism of Marx and Engels is tainted with mechanical determinism and fatalism, none of which is intended in historical materialism. The other bias is to over-emphasize the subjectivity and purposiveness of social development, but consciously or unconsciously ignore or deny the objectivity and regularity of social development. Consequently, historical materialism is contaminated with voluntarism and historical idealism. In fact, the founders of historical materialism have discussed not only the objectivity and regularity of historical development, but also the subjectivity and purposiveness of it, and offered a proper combination of the two.[2] The "development of social forms" is equivalent in meaning to "social development." And the proposition of "the unity between the regularity and the purposiveness of social development" may not represent my true intentions.

First, the claim of "the regularity of social development" is untenable. I initially made this claim to explain that "there are laws in the process of social development." However, it does not mean that social development itself has a regular pattern, but that there are laws governing human development in its different stages, laws that await in need of our discovery. Therefore, social development and development laws are two separate entities. Likewise, the claim of "the purposiveness of social development" is also untenable. My original intention behind this claim was that "there are purposes in human activities," not to mean that people's activities may render purposeful results, but that there are purposes outside the society and its development, waiting or needing us to discover and comply with them. The above claim conveys certain teleology of idealism. The proposition of "the unity between the regularity and the purposiveness of social development" should be revised as "there are purposes in human activities and there are laws in social development," to truly capture my intention.

Second, the aforesaid proposition not only fails to express my original meaning, but unconsciously conveys a wrong historical view. Semantically, the proposition of "the unity between the regularity and the purposiveness of social development" argues that the regularity of social development is consistent with the purpose of human activities. However, we know that in historical development, individuals' activities are indeed purposeful, but the social results produced by interactions of purposeful activities of countless individuals are not completely consistent with and are even antithetical to an individual's own purpose. This is necessarily so because social development has its objective laws independent of human will and purpose. Therefore, it is a perspective of historical idealism to claim that the regularity of social development is consistent with the purposiveness of human activities.

In my book *A Course in Marxist Philosophy* co-authored with Nie Jinfang and Zhang Libo, the proposition of "the unity between the regularity and the purposiveness of social development" is revised into "the purposiveness and regularity of human activities." I made the following explanations on this revision:

> Idealists' regularity and purposiveness for historical development differs completely from historical materialists' regularity and purposiveness for human activities. The former attempts to address the relationship among historical regularity, progressiveness, and free will, based on historicism and the whole of history. Such is seen, for instance, in Vico, Kant, and Hegel. To these philosophers, an individual's unique activities often appear purposeless. Their activities with their own unique purposes are often the instrumentality used by God, Nature, and Rationality for the latter's infinite purpose.

Therefore, to these philosophers, there exists unity between the regularity and the purposiveness of historical development. The historical materialists' contention, on the other hand, concerns the "fulfilled person" and "material production." To Marx and Engels, "society" and "history" are not abstract, but specific human activities in a specific society of a specific production mode. Regularity and purposiveness mean that human activities are conscious and purposeful, unlike animalistic instinct. This regularity and purposiveness, however, are nonexistent in social and historical development.[3]

Although my book has pointed out that the proposition of the "unity between the regularity and the purposiveness of the social historical process" is historical idealism, "regularity and purposiveness are nonexistent in social development" from the perspective of historical materialism. This historical materialism perspective helps correct inadequacies in my book. However, the proposition of "the purposiveness and the regularity of human activities" remains uncorrected. The claim of "the purposiveness of human activities" implies an idealistic teleology for historical development and is thus fallacious. Human activities may either follow or violate the laws of social development. The "regularity of human activities" may lead to the illusion that human activities and the laws of social development are separate from each other, that the latter are independently before and above human activities, waiting to be followed, abided by, and achieved in human activities. In reality, however, social laws are exactly also laws of human social activities, and stand inseparable from the latter.

A Course in Historical Materialism is rated as a key national-level college textbook in social sciences for the "Ninth Five-Year Plan." *A Course in Marxist Philosophy* is rated as a key textbook for the "Tenth Five-Year Plan" by the Ministry of Education, and as quality college textbook by the City of Beijing. Both books have seen over ten prints from the press. With wide readership and extensive influence, the negative effects from errors and inaccuracies therein are serious. After becoming aware of this, I have attempted every correction to confine the negative effects. I have also sincerely apologized to my readers, including teachers, students, and the general public.

2.2 The proposition of "the purposiveness of social development" is a view of historical teleology

Human activities are conscious and purposeful. It is such activities that have created the history of human society. Without human activities, there would be no human history. Marx repeatedly and highly praised Vico, father of historical philosophy, for the latter's opinion that "history is made by ourselves."[4] However, Vico means that neither social history nor human society develops in accordance with humans' purposes. The claim of "purposiveness" in the development of social history is incompatible with historical materialism. It conveys the teleological view of historical idealism, a view prevalent before the establishment of historical materialism. Historical teleology is an "idealism—an expression of the purposiveness of history—that holds that the process of history is determined by a certain purpose."[5] Historical teleology originated in ancient Greece and Rome, where Socrates believes that in historical development, "the soul" is God, arranging and controlling everything, and that human activities must conform to God's purposes. Plato believes that "idea" is the essence of everything, "the highest good" is the supreme idea, and social development and social hierarchy are subject to the purpose of "the highest good." Seeking virtue over vice is a common feature of historical teleology. Below is a brief introduction of major representatives of historical teleology.

The City of God by Augustine (354–430), a Christian philosopher in Ancient Greece, is a work of theological teleology. Augustine believes that after Adam committed the original sin, the world has been dichotomized into the city of God and that of secularity. The inhabitants of the former are believers of God, while those of the latter are ruled by Satan the devil. These two different cities practice two different kinds of "love." To Augustine, the entire human history witnesses two kinds of conflicts. The first is between the city of God and the city of secularity. This conflict is rooted in two different kinds of love seen in the two cities. In the city of God, love is dedicated to God and above the self, whereas in the city of secularity, love is self-love or selfish love that disdains God. These two different kinds of love breed continuous strife between the two cities. The second type of conflict is internal within the city of secularity, attributable to human selfishness and embodied in mutual subjugation and antagonism among humans in their pursuit of personal interests. Augustine thinks that human history is full of struggles between believers of God and those of Satan. As a result, humans constantly move toward the paradise of God while the devil's followers are cast into hell. The city of God finally replaces the city of secularity, and believers of God eventually enter into the heaven of happiness, fulfilling the purpose of God.

Italian philosopher Giovanni Battista Vico (1668–1774) also holds the view of historical teleology. Vico believes that humans have free will.

> But men, because of their corrupted nature, are under the tyranny of self-love, which compels them to make private utility their chief guide. Seeking everything useful for themselves and nothing for their companions, they cannot bring their passions under control to direct them toward justice.

Therefore, the presence of a certain god becomes necessary. With His providence, God controls selfish human passions, which He transforms into virtues. Omnipotent and unlimited in wisdom as governor, God can establish His institutions by means as easy as natural human customs, and bring human activities under His institutive order. Vico also argues that since the divine providence "has for its end its own immeasurable goodness, whatever it institutes must be directed to a good always superior to that which men have proposed to themselves."[6] Hence, everyone pursues his or her own special purposes and interests, but they would always unconsciously fulfill the purpose designed by the divine providence.

Immanuel Kant (1724–1804) holds a similar view to Giovanni Battista Vico. Kant believes that nature endows people with two basic sentiments. The first is egoism and individualism; the second, altruism and collectivism. When the first dominates, the human is radically evil. This evil drives people to their own interests, propelling history in a corresponding direction. Altruism, however, restricts the rampage of egoism. The contradictions between egoism and altruism and the solutions thereof drive historical progress. Kant says:

> Each, according to his own inclination, follows his own purpose, often in opposition to others; yet each individual and people, as if following some guiding thread, go toward a natural but to each of them unknown goal; all work toward furthering it, even if they would set little store by it if they did know it.[7]

According to Kant, the natural goal guides or forces people to go in a direction prescribed by nature's intentions; it first makes people's evil natures inspire their various gifts, discover their various potentialities, and motivate them to fight. After suffering the pain and catastrophes caused by blind forces of the evil nature, people sober up to the idea that they must get rid of the savagery of evils and deception to create a civil society via legal restrictions. That is to say, although people are designing their own special plans and pursuing their own special interests, they, as a matter of fact, are manipulated by nature and are led to goals prescribed by nature. Individuals, and even entire nations, are seldom aware that they are unconsciously realizing natural intentions when each follows its own purpose according to its own inclination even in opposition to others'. In short, Kant regards the evil of human nature as an important leverage for historical progress. Evil is the direct impetus for historical development and the tool to achieve goodness. The ultimate goal of history, however, is goodness. The trajectory of development is to achieve goodness through evil.

G. W. F. Hegel (1770–1831) has a teleological perspective similar to Vico and Kant. Hegel believes that the individual is a special entity. The individual's power to act comes from his will, closely linked with his self-desire. The self-desire of egoism arouses enthusiasm. Although Hegel believes that selfish and wicked desires directly propel historical development, he also believes that the enthusiasm inspired by selfish desires must be controlled by reason. Seeing only phenomena and with limited consciousness, human actions and history are a series of passionate impulsions and activities; however, in terms of nature and infinite reason, they are also activities of rationality. Reason is so cunning that it uses human enthusiasm as a tool to achieve its end. Hegel said in *The Shorter Logic*:

> Reason is as *cunning* as it is *powerful*. Cunning may be said to lie in the intermediate action which, while it permits the objects to follow their own bent and act upon one another till they waste away, and does not itself directly interfere in the process, is nevertheless only working out *its own* aims. With this explanation, Divine Providence may be said to stand to the world and its

process in the capacity of absolute cunning. God lets men do as they please with their particular passions and interests; but the result is the accomplishment of - not their plans, but *his*, and these differ decidedly from the ends primarily sought by those whom he employs.[8]

Hegel argues that selfish desires, passion, and enthusiasm are the exterior and direct driving forces for historical development, and reason is the deep-rooted driving force for it.

2.3 Marx and Engels' critique of historical teleology

Marx and Engels, founders of historical materialism, always have a critical attitude towards historical teleology. Engels criticized the teleology of theology in his article *The Condition of England: A Review of Past and Present by Thomas Carlyle*, written October 1843 to January 1844. At the time, he was still influenced by Ludwig Andreas Feuerbach's humanism, and his critique of theology's historical teleology was also affected by it. Engels pointed out:

> We have no intention whatever of doubting or despising the "revelation of history", for history is all and everything to us and we hold it more highly than any other previous philosophical trend, more highly than Hegel even, who after all used it only as a case against which to test his logical problem.

Engels believed that it is not we but Christians who scorn history and disregard the development of mankind. They create a separate "history of the Kingdom of God" and deny the inner substantiality of real history. "We lay claim to the meaning of history, but we see in history not the revelation of 'God' but of man and only of man." In order to see the splendor of the human character, to recognize the development of human species through history, its irresistible progress, its ever certain victory over the unreason of the individual, its hard but successful struggle against nature until the final achievement of free human self-consciousness, the discernment of the unity of man and nature, and the independent creation—voluntarily and by its own effort—of a new world based on purely human and moral social relationships,

> [i]n order to recognize all that in its greatness, we have no need first to summon up the abstraction of a "God" and to attribute to it everything beautiful, great, sublime and truly human; we do not need to follow this roundabout path, we do not need first to imprint the stamp of the "divine" on what is truly human, in order to be sure of its greatness and splendor.[9]

Engels means that we should not attribute all the great achievements and beautiful things created by human in history to the realization of God's purposes. Although Engels had not completely transformed into a historical materialist at the time, he confirmedly opposed theological teleology. In the book *The Holy Family* written on the eve of the formation of historical materialism, Marx and Engels criticized the historical teleology of the young Hegelian Bruno Bauer. Marx and Engels severely rebuked Bauer's view that the mission of history is to prove to oneself the truth that she/he has been aware of:

> Just as, according to the earlier teleologists, plants exist to be eaten by animals, and animals to be eaten by men, history exists in order to serve as the act of consumption of theoretical eating - proving. Man exists so that history may exist, and history exists so that the *proof of truths* exists. In this *critically* trivialized form is repeated the speculative wisdom that man exists, and history exists, so that *truth may arrive at self-consciousness.*[10]

Bauer's point of view was derived completely from Hegel's conception of history. Marx and Engels argued:

> *Hegel*'s conception of history presupposes an abstract or absolute spirit which develops in such a way that mankind is a mere *mass* that bears the spirit with a varying degree of consciousness or unconsciousness. Within *empirical*, exoteric history, therefore, Hegel makes a *speculative*, esoteric history develop. The history of mankind becomes the history of the *abstract spirit* of mankind, hence *a spirit far removed* from the real man.[11]

When Bauer declaimed "the real wealth of human relations, the immense content of history, the struggle of history, the fight of the mass against the spirit," Marx and Engels criticized:

> *History does nothing*, it "possesses *no* immense wealth", it "wages *no* battles". It is *man*, real, living man who does all that, who possesses and fights; "history" is not, as it were, a person apart, using *man* as a means to achieve *its* own aims; history is *nothing but* the activities of man pursuing *his* aims.[12]

In a letter to Pavel Vasilyevich Annenkov on December 28, 1846, Marx criticized Proudhon's historical teleology. Proudhon confused thoughts and things and did not understand the actual process of historical development. Therefore, like Hegel, he talked about God, universal reason, and human beings dominating the world without reason. In this regard, Marx pointed out that Proudhon's

> history takes place in the nebulous realm of the imagination and soars high above time and place. In a word, it is Hegelian trash, it is not history, it is not profane history—history of mankind, but sacred history—history of ideas. As seen by him, man is but the instrument used by the idea of eternal reason in order to unfold itself.[13]

In his manuscript *Dialectics of Nature* written in his late years, Engels criticized the teleological viewpoints in natural science when discussing the development of natural science in the first half of the 18th century. He said:

The highest general idea to which this natural science attained was that of the purposiveness of the arrangements of nature, the shallow teleology of Wolff, according to which cats were created to eat mice, mice to be eaten by cats, and the whole of nature to testify to the wisdom of the creator.[14]

Marx and Engels, as unwavering critics of historical teleology, would never consider historical development a purposeful process. The view of the "purposiveness" of social historical development is not that of historical materialism founded by Marx and Engels and should be removed from textbooks of historical materialism and Marxist philosophy.

2.4 The purpose of human activities is not equivalent to the "purposiveness" of social development

As now apparent to our comprehension, the development of history is for achieving neither the purpose of some deity or God nor the intent of another celestial being, of nature, or of design of reason. Is the development of history aiming to achieve—and thus in line with—the purpose of people in the real world? Of course not.

Historical materialism holds that human activities are conscious and purposeful. It is such activities that have created human history. Human society itself, let alone its history, cannot emerge absent of these activities. Why then can't we claim that the development of history is in line with the purpose of the human? Simply put, why can't we claim the "purposiveness" of the development of social history? This indeed is a theoretical issue in historical studies worthy of further elaboration. Our past investigation was not thorough or incisive. Marx and Engels did claim that human activities are conscious and purposeful. However, they also claimed that development of social history is not subject to human will or purpose. Indeed, they never proposed a "purposiveness" for the development of social history. They never advocated but actually opposed "historical teleology." What follows is a systematic investigation and elucidation of Marx and Engels on this issue.

In *Capital Volume I*, Marx said:

> We pre-suppose labour in a form that stamps it as exclusively human. A spider conducts operations that resemble those of a weaver, and a bee puts to shame many an architect in the construction of her cells. But what distinguishes the worst architect from the best of bees is this, that the architect raises his structure in imagination before he erects it in reality. At the end of every labour-process, we get a result that already existed in the imagination of the labourer at its commencement. He not only effects a change of form in the material on which he works, but he also realizes a purpose of his own that gives the law to his modus operandi, and to which he must subordinate his will.[15]

Marx's remarks are about the characteristics of human activities and the differences between human activities and animal activities. Animal activities are instinctive and unconscious. Animals do not have self-consciousness and are not able to regard themselves as subjects and their activities as objects. They cannot conceive a purpose in their activities; human activities are conscious and purposeful. Humans have self-consciousness and are able to regard themselves as the subjects and their activities as objects. They can consciously realize the purpose of their activities. The purpose put forward by a human as a historical subject restricts his entire activity process. The subject uses requisite material forces and means to act upon the external object in accordance with a certain purpose, so that the object changes per his own purpose and the subject realizes his purpose to meet his various needs. Thus, we can claim that human activities are a process where one tends to achieve the purpose of the subject in an orderly manner, or that, in Marx's words, one's purpose "gives the law" to one's modus operandi.

Why, then, can't we claim a "purposiveness" for social historical development in spite of all our arguments mentioned before and seen immediately hereafter? Those human activities are conscious and purposeful. It is conscious and purposeful human activities that have created their own history and its development laws. Those historical subjects enable historical objects to change in accordance with the former's own purposes. That subject's purpose "gives the law" to his/her modus operandi. On this issue, Marx and Engels have offered explanations from multiple perspectives.

First, since people of conscious and purposeful activities, in the process of their history and their interactions, affect, constrain, interfere with, hinder, and outbalance each other, the ultimate result of history stays in the control of no particular subject. In *Ludwig Feuerbach and the End of Classical German Philosophy*, Engels says:

> Men make their own history, whatever its outcome may be, in that each person follows his own consciously desired end, and it is precisely the resultant of these many wills operating in different directions, and of their manifold effects upon the outer world, that constitutes history. Thus it is also a question of what the many individuals desire. The will is determined by passion or deliberation. But the levers which immediately determine passion or deliberation are of very different kinds. Partly they may be external objects, partly ideal motives, ambition, "enthusiasm for truth and justice", personal hatred, or even purely individual whims of all kinds. But, on the one hand, we have seen that the many individual wills active in history for the most part produce results quite other than those intended—often quite the opposite; that their motives, therefore, in relation to the total result are likewise of only secondary importance.[16]

Engels made this point clearer in *Letter to Joseph Bloch (Engels)* in September 1890. He pointed out:

> History is made in such a way that the final result always arises from conflicts between many individual wills, of which each in turn has been made what it

is by a host of particular conditions of life. Thus there are innumerable inter-secting forces, an infinite series of parallelograms of forces which give rise to one resultant—the historical event. This may again itself be viewed as the product of a power which works as a whole unconsciously and without voli-tion. For what each individual will is obstructed by everyone else, and what emerges is something that no one willed. Thus history has proceeded hitherto in the manner of a natural process and is essentially subject to the same laws of motion. But from the fact that the wills of individuals—do not attain what they want, but are merged into an aggregate mean, a common resultant, it must not be concluded that they are equal to zero. On the contrary, each con-tributes to the resultant and is to this extent included in it.[17]

By revealing the relationship between the desired ends and wills of individuals and the resultant (outcome of history) engendered by these wills and desired ends, Engels, as previously quoted, demonstrates that though each individual's activi-ties are conscious and purposeful and each individual of conscious and purposeful activities makes contributions to the outcome of history, the outcome of historical development does not proceed according to the will and purpose of any individual. This profoundly explains why development of social history is not "purposive."

Second, as people's conscious and purposeful activities are conditioned by objective conditions, if the former goes against the latter, human activities may not achieve the desired end, and may even incur the opposite. This kind of situation is often seen in human activities that transform nature and society. In *Dialectics of Nature*, Engels says that people should follow objective laws to harness and transform nature. If it is solely for our needs that we ceaselessly exploit and waste nature's resources in violation of nature's law, we will fail to achieve the desired end and will certainly be punished by nature. He pointed out:

> Let us not, however, flatter ourselves overmuch on account of our human conquest over nature. For each such conquest takes its revenge on us. Each of them, it is true, has in the first place the consequences on which we counted, but in the second and third places it has quite different, unforeseen effects which only too often cancel out the first.[18]

To illustrate, Engels offered numerous examples.

> People who, in Mesopotamia, Greece, Asia Minor, and elsewhere, destroyed the forests to obtain cultivable land, never dreamed that they were laying the basis for the present devastated condition of these countries, by remov-ing along with the forests the collecting centres and reservoirs of moisture. When, on the southern slopes of the mountains, the Italians of the Alps used up the pine forests so carefully cherished on the northern slopes, they had no inkling that by doing so they were cutting at the roots of the dairy industry in their region; they had still less inkling that they were thereby depriving their mountain springs of water for the greater part of the year, with the effect that

these would be able to pour still more furious flood torrents on the plains during the rainy seasons. Those who spread the potato in Europe were not aware that they were at the same time spreading the disease of scrofula.

Engels derives valuable lessons from above examples:

> We by no means rule over nature like a conqueror over a foreign people, like someone standing outside nature - but that we, with flesh, blood, and brain, belong to nature, and exist in its midst, and that all our mastery of it consists in the fact that we have the advantage over all other beings of being able to know and correctly apply its laws.[19]

Engels thus has demonstrated that people's historical activities in changing the world are conscious and purposeful, but since these activities are conditioned by objective conditions, the outcomes of the activities may not always be what they desired. This also explains why development of social history is not "purposive."

Third, since our conscious and purposeful activities are at mercy not only of objective conditions but also of subjective conditions (our cognitive ability and practice), the outcomes of human activities may fully, partially, or not at all accomplish the desired end; they may also produce the opposite of what is desired. For a start, our knowledge and practice are restricted by historical conditions. Engels pointed out: "We can only know under the conditions of our epoch and as far as these allow."[20] And human understanding is forever premised upon the contradiction between the supremacy and non-supremacy, between infiniteness and finiteness, and between absoluteness and relativity, of our process of cognition. As a result, the outcomes of people's thinking (i.e., understanding of the external world) will contain both truth and fallacy. A careful review of human history may likely reveal more fallacy than truth. The same may apply to a cautious projection into our future—more mistakes may be made than by our predecessors. As Engels says:

> Inasmuch as all probability we are just about at the beginning of human history, and the generations which will put us right are likely to be far more numerous than those whose knowledge we—often enough with a considerable degree of contempt—have the opportunity to correct.

Supremacy of thinking is based on the understanding of multiple generations of humankind. As for each individual, his or her understanding is without supremacy. Again as Engels says:

> But as for the sovereign validity of the knowledge obtained by each individual thought, we all know that there can be no talk of such a thing, and that all previous experience shows that without exception such knowledge always contains much more that is capable of being improved upon than that which cannot be improved upon, or is correct.[21]

Again, everyone's cognition is premised on their own subjective conditions such as family status, education, knowledge, and practical skills. People's subjective conditions have both strengths and weaknesses. A perfect and all-powerful individual is nonexistent. Due to the above restrictions, it is not possible for the desired end of people to be completely correct or completely realizable. This shows again that the development of social history is not "purposive."

Fourth, historical materialism sees the development of society as a natural process governed by objective laws independent of human will. People's conscious and purposeful activities can only extend or shorten the historical process to a certain extent, increase or reduce the suffering that history brings upon humans, but human activities cannot "skip or order to cancel the development of nature."[22] If people's conscious and purposeful activities fully reach their desired ends, history then develops in full accordance with the wills and purposes of the human actor. In this case, historical development will have no objective laws independent of human will and purpose. We know, however, that this does not depict how human participation in history actually unfolds. At least up to now, participants in history have not formed a concerted purpose. Then what constitutes the basis of historical development? Most previous views hold that history is based on the purposes, thoughts, and intentions of geniuses and heroes. In *Anti-Duhring* Engels thus summarized the idealistic historical views of the three great utopian socialists in the 19th century (Owen, Saint-Simon, and Fourier):

> [T]hey wish to bring in the kingdom of reason and eternal justice, but this kingdom, as they see it, is as far as heaven from earth, from that of the French philosophers. For the bourgeois world, based upon the principles of these philosophers, is quite as irrational and unjust, and, therefore, finds its way to the dust-hole quite as readily as feudalism and all the earlier stages of society. If pure reason and justice have not, hitherto, ruled the world, this has been the case only because men have not rightly understood them. What was wanted was the individual man of genius, who has now arisen and who understands the truth. That he has now arisen, that the truth has now been clearly understood, is not an inevitable event, following of necessity in the chain of historical development, but a mere happy accident. He might just as well have been born 500 years earlier, and might then have spared humanity 500 years of error, strife, and suffering.[23]

The historical idealism, as cited above, sees the development of social history as "purposive" where only contingency determines the wills, purposes, thoughts, and intentions of figures and geniuses in history.

Here, we should make it explicit again that the development of social history is not "purposive." This is not to deny that people's activities are conscious and purposeful or to advocate blind and purposeless activities. Human activities *are* conscious and purposeful, a fundamental and undeniable feature distinguishing human activities from those of animals. We offer the following substantiations. (1) Development of social history is objective. It has objective laws independent of human wills and purposes. We must treat our plans and designs (even our top-level ones) for social development with equanimity, and constantly adjust them according to the actual situation. No matter how scientific and thoughtful our planning and design are, they may fail in actual execution. This has been corroborated by practice. (2) People's conscious and purposeful activities are premised on objective conditions. Goals that conform to objective conditions are more likely to materialize; those that go against objective conditions are less likely or even impossible to materialize. When setting the purpose of our activities, we must fully understand, conform our goals toward, or adjust our goals according to the objective conditions. (3) People's conscious and purposeful activities are confined by subjective conditions. Goals that conform to subjective conditions are more likely to be achieved, and those that go against subjective conditions are less likely or even impossible to be achieved. When we set the goal of our activities, we must endeavor to understand and conform our goals to our subjective conditions. In cases where such conformity is absent, we must promptly adjust our goals. We must not reach for what is beyond the grasp of our subjective conditions. In this respect, we have learned bitter lessons in the past. (4) Even if our goals meet objective and subjective conditions, we may not be able to achieve them. For actors of conscious and purposeful activities, their wills, purposes, and strengths influence, interact with, and restrict each other. If each individual's will, purpose, and strength accord, mutually promote, and complement each other, their goals are more likely to be achieved. However, if they are mutually exclusive, contradict, and interfere with each other, the possibility of achievement is comparatively small or absent. When we set the goal of our activities, we must consider its interaction with that of others, the complex social environment and interpersonal relationships, and the dynamic changes therein.

2.5 The proposition that "social development has laws" is incompatible with the nature and characteristics of the laws of social history

The development of social history has objective laws independent of human wills. This is the basic view of historical materialism. Why then can't we claim that the development of social history "has laws"? This entails the understanding of a series of important issues such as the characteristics, nature, formation, and implementation of the laws of social history.

First, the law of social history is the law of human activities. It is inherent within rather than prior to or above humans' historical activities. As mentioned above, the development law of human society is fundamentally different from that of nature. Disregarding people's reaction to the natural world, we will find that the development and changes of the natural world are blind and unconscious. The law of natural development is manifested and realized through the interaction among these blind and unconscious forces. However, the development of human social history is different. Human activities are conscious and purposeful, constituting the history and law of human society. The law of social history is the law of human social activities.

In this sense, the law of social history is also a product of the subject's historical practice. Prior to and outside of the practice of the human subject, there is no creator of social history or of the law of social history. Moreover, it is impossible for the law of human social development to be realized spontaneously; it needs to be realized through humans' conscious and purposeful activities. Without these activities, there would be no history of human society, nor law of human social history. The claim that social history is law-governed essentially separates the law of social history from humans' practical activities and from the development of social history. It may seem that the law of social history exists independently prior to and outside of the practice of humans and the development processes of social history, awaiting the latter to follow it, to comply with it, and to realize it. Originally, people want to express the basic viewpoint of historical materialism through the claim that law governs the development of social history. Semantically, however, the above claim signifies the *a priori* preconception of historical idealism. Therefore, this claim must be revised as the "regularity" of social development.

Second, the laws of social history are historic. Different social and historical rules exist in different historical periods. There is no eternal social history rule. In the afterword of the second edition of *Capital*, Marx quoted Ilarion Ignatyevich Kaufman on the nature of the law of social development. Kaufman said:

> But it will be said, the general laws of economic life are one and the same, no matter whether they are applied to the present or the past. This Marx directly denies. According to him, such abstract laws do not exist ... On the contrary, in his opinion every historical period has laws of its own ... As soon as society has outlived a given period of development, and is passing over from one given stage to another, it begins to be subject also to other laws.

For example,

> Marx denies that the law of population is the same at all times and in all places. He asserts, on the contrary, that every stage of development has its own law of population ... With the varying degree of development of productive power, social conditions and the laws governing them vary too.[24]

Marx fully affirmed and highly praised Kaufman's view. According to Marx and Kaufman, if a social form exists, the law of it will exist and operate. If an old social form is replaced by a new one, the old social form will cease and step down from the stage of history. Accordingly, the law in the old social form will be replaced by the law of the new social form. If the history of human society is one of successive replacement of social patterns, it will also be the history of replacement in the law of social development, where the new law of a new period replaces that of an old period.

In his letter to Friedrich Albert Lange on March 29, 1865, Engels criticized the view of bourgeois economists on the permanence of the law of capitalist economy. He said:

To us, so-called economic laws are not eternal laws of nature but historic laws which arise and disappear ... To us also, therefore, none of these laws, in so far as it expresses purely bourgeois conditions, is older than modern bourgeois society; those which have hitherto been more or less valid throughout all history only express just those relations which are common to the conditions of all society based on class rule and class exploitation. To the former belongs the so-called law of Ricardo, which is valid neither for feudal serfdom nor ancient slavery, to the latter belongs what is tenable in the so-called Malthusian theory.[25]

Marx wrote *Capital* to clarify the law of the capitalist economic movement. The basic idea of the whole book is to oppose the stereotypes of bourgeois economists who regard economic law as permanent. In his first review for *Capital Volume I*, Engels discussed this viewpoint incisively. He said:

We must confess that we are much impressed by the sense of history which pervades the whole book and forbids the author to take the laws of economics for eternal truths, for anything but the formulations of the conditions of existence of certain transitory states of society; we would, alas, look in vain among our official economists for that scholarship and acumen with which the various historical states of society and their conditions of existence are here presented. Studies like that on the economic conditions and laws of slavery, the various forms of serfdom and bondage and the origin of free labour have hitherto remained quite alien to our economic specialists.[26]

The above observation indicates that both Marx and Engels think that the law of social history is historic and oppose the idea that the law of development of any social form, especially that of the capitalist society, is eternal. Semantically, the claim of "governance by law" in the development of social history is not only unable to express the historicity of social law, but easily leads to the eternity of it.

Third, the law of social history has a character of indirect reality. It cannot be presented to people directly and is mastered only through abstract thinking. It is not in full conformity with objective reality at any time or under any circumstance. Conrad Schmidt believes that the economic law is only an assumption and fiction because he finds no complete consistency between objective reality and economic laws (such as the laws of value and of average profit rate). Engels, in his letter of March 12, 1895 to Conrad Schmidt, was clearly critical of Schmidt's above theory. Engels argued that law of average rate of profit at any moment

only exists approximately. If it were for once realized in two undertakings down to the last jot and dot, if both resulted in exactly the same rate of profit in a given year, that would be pure accident; in reality the rates of profit vary from business to business and from year to year according to different circumstances, and the general rate only exists as an average of many businesses and a series of years. But if we were to demand the rate of profit—say

14.876934…—[it] should be exactly similar in every business and every year down to the 100th decimal place, on pain of degradation to fiction, we should be grossly misunderstanding the nature of the rate of profit and of economic laws in general—none of them has any reality except as approximation, tendency, average, and not as immediate reality. This is due partly to the fact that their action clashes with the simultaneous action of other laws, but partly to their own nature as concepts.[27]

In other words, the law of social history is neither direct nor a direct reality, for two reasons:

First, numerous laws in human society may exist and operate simultaneously. The function of one law is affected by other laws. For example, the law that value determines price is influenced by many other laws such as those of supply and demand, income distribution, tax, fiscal and monetary conditions, finance, industrial structure change, and international trade, etc. Therefore, the price is neither consistent nor an exact match with the value on any particular occasion, but fluctuates around value through price. Only in aggregated average, price may approximate value. Marx continued:

> In capitalist production as a whole "the general law maintains itself as the governing tendency" only in a very complex and approximate manner, as the constantly changing average of perpetual fluctuations.[28]

For another example, in the absence of other laws and social factors, relations of production operate in tandem with the nature of the productive forces. In the complexity of reality, however, production relations are at the mercy of so many other social laws and factors: The geographical environment and its changes, demographics, class struggle in a class society, superstructure and its need to follow economic development, international relations and environment, fiscal and monetary policies, world finance and currency system, etc. Consequently, the relationship between productive relations and productivity could be variously skewed, and they consequently lose the perfect correlation with each other. In countries with the same level of productivity, different production relations may emerge, while in countries with different levels of productivity, the same production relations may emerge. It may even be possible to achieve higher production relations in countries with lower productivity, and vice versa. This situation is quite obvious in the current world.

Second, the laws of social history are latent behind social and historical phenomena. They are not directly visible but need to be deduced through abstract logical thinking. They are conceptual in nature and, *prima facie*, not identical or congruent with immediate reality. Engels says:

> The concept of a thing and its reality, run side by side like two asymptotes, always approaching each other but never meeting. This difference between the two is the very difference which prevents the concept from being directly

and immediately reality and reality from being immediately its own concept. But although a concept has the essential nature of a concept and cannot therefore prima facie directly coincide with reality.[29]

There is no doubt that no concept is pure imagination but is abstracted from historical reality. However, any concept, being abstracted from reality, loses the details, nuances, and serendipities embedded in the conceptualized reality. Reality is always more complex than the concept of that reality. The concept is always only a simplified clarification of the reality.

Semantically, the claim of "governance by law" in the development of social history not only fails to reflect the non-immediacy of this law, but also leads to a mechanical understanding of this law as *a priori* that operates outside of concrete historicity. The famous British philosopher of science Karl Popper mentioned in his book *The Poverty of Historicism* that "laws and trends are fundamentally different things." To Popper, "the existence of trends is undoubted" and there is no possibility of a "law of social movement."[30] Popper's argument may represent a mechanical understanding of the law which he equates with a direct and immediate reality. To a dialectical view of the laws of social history, the law is only a tendency rather than a concrete reality.

Fourth, the law of social history is procedural. Its gestation, formation, operation, and eventual materialization are a long, coherent, and holistic process, which cannot be fragmented. That is, no law of social form, before its final materialization, can yet be regarded as complete and fully formed. Let's look at the law that socialism will inevitably replace capitalism. As long as capitalism is still operative and socialism is not yet victorious, it cannot be said that this law has been fully formed. Globally at present, capitalism will stay for quite some time to come. No one can accurately predict the time when it will be replaced by socialism. It is also difficult to foretell how capitalism will develop in the future and what specific changes will occur. The concrete form in which socialism replaces capitalism can only be determined on the basis of specific future conditions. In short, before the actual replacement of capitalism by socialism, the law that socialism will inevitably replace capitalism is not fully materialized. Once materialized, the law disappears from history, yielding to new laws of the socialist society and the communist society. The primitive society had been extremely long. The slavery society had existed for about a thousand years before being replaced by the feudal society. The feudal society had existed for more than a thousand years before being replaced by the capitalist society. Theorists disagree whether China went through a slave society or not, but that is not our focus here. The feudal society had existed in China for over 2,000 years. After the Opium War in 1840, China gradually shifted to a semi-colonial and semi-feudal society. The Chinese Communist Party led the people of all ethnic groups into a new socialist democracy after a long bloody fight.

Now we have given our example of socialism's replacement of capitalism to illustrate that the gestation, formation, operation, and final realization of the law that one social form replaces another are long, coherent, and holistic. Does this apply to specific laws within a specific social form? We will use some of the specific laws in a capitalist society for illustration. Major laws governing capitalism include those of the circulation of money, of value, of residual value, of average rate of profit, of the downward tendency of the general rate of profit, of diminishing fertility of the soil, of competition and anarchy of capitalist production, of the imbalance in economic and political development of capitalist countries, and of economic and financial crisis. Unlike the law that governs the replacement of one social form by another, the manifestation of laws within one social form do not need to go through complete replacement of one social form by another. Instead, such latter laws are manifested through constant periodic swings within the same social form. However, each cycle of swing may also be a protracted process. As long as the social form in which these laws operate remains alive, the constant periodic swings remain active, each swing of distinct traits. This can be explicitly demonstrated by the swings in the law of value and the law of average rate of profit, and by the cycle of the four phases of the capitalistic economic crisis (namely crisis, depression, resuscitation, and upsurge). Many economic theories explain the swings of capitalism. As this is not our focus, no further discussion concerning this will be offered.

The claim of the "regularity" of the historical development of society, semantically, may not accurately express the fact that the gestation, formation, operation, and final realization of the law of social history are a long-term, coherent, and holistic process. Furthermore, the claim fragments the above process by contending that the law of social development, once materialized, becomes reified in the presence of social actors for the latter to simply discover, follow, and fulfill. Karl Popper objected to Karl Marx's opinion regarding the objective regularity in the historical development of society. The objection arises because Popper distorted or at least misunderstood Marx. Consequently, to Popper, the law of social history remains permanent and immutable the moment it takes shape since it's an *a priori* and isolated existence independent of actual social conditions and changes. In his *The Poverty of Historicism*, Popper claims,

> If we were to admit laws that are themselves subject to change, change could never be explained by laws. It would be the admission that change is simply miraculous.[31]

2.6 Correctly understanding "act according to objective laws"

The law of social history is conceptual and logical, encapsulating the inherent, essential, and inevitable connections embedded in phenomena. Therefore, comprehension of the law is not immediate but entails abstract thinking. The law, in its logical conceptualization, represents only an approximation, a tendency, or an average as opposed to immediate and direct reality. This challenges the effort to comprehend and master the law of social history. In other words, in the field of social history, it is never easy to actually act in accordance with the objective laws.

People are undoubtedly correct when they opine that "we should respect the objective laws" and "we must act in accordance with the objective laws."

However, for a long time, people have made rather simple and even incorrect interpretations here. They tend to view the laws of social history as a pre-existence long before and external to human activities. It may seem that the moment a certain social form is born, its developmental laws come along. The laws are already out there awaiting people to recognize, respect, realize, and comply with them. This view neglects and denies, consciously or unconsciously, the feature that logically conceptualized laws can only be "approximations, tendencies, or averages, as opposed to immediate facts." But what are the correct interpretations of these terms? According to Marx and Engels, laws are the necessary trends of development actuated by contradictions within things; they are neither direct facts nor physical products. They are invisible and intangible. Comprehension of laws requires long, diligent, and comprehensive investigation and research on a massive scale of phenomena. As Marx puts in the preface to his *Capital Volume I*, "In the analysis of economic forms, moreover, neither microscopes nor chemical reagents are of use. The force of abstraction must replace both."[32] By "respecting the objective laws" and "acting in accordance with the objective laws," Marx means that people's understanding and action must follow the inherent contradictions of things and the consequent trends of development and their predictions of such. In the field of social history, "acting in accordance with the objective laws" is never an obviously imitative operation like architectural construction per blueprints or calligraphy through tracing. It is a complicated process requiring acute cognition and practice. First of all, due to objective laws' long process of gestation, formation, operation, and realization, their revelation to us can only be gradual. There is no way for people to recognize them—before their full manifestation—let alone act in accordance with them. Second, though relatively stable and iterative, objective laws can be fickle in their manifestations. Human recognition forever lags behind the objective laws. Although we may enrich and deepen our comprehension of laws, that comprehension forever remains but an approximation rather than complete reflection of objective laws. Moreover, the manifestations of objective laws vary with time, making it necessary to constantly adjust our understanding of the laws. Ossified and dogmatic understandings will not enable us to "act according to objective laws." In the Preface to *Capital Volume III*, Engels said,

> Where things and their interrelations are conceived, not as fixed, but as changing, their mental images, the ideas, are likewise subject to change and transformation; and they are not encapsulated in rigid definitions, but are developed in their historical or logical process of formation.[33]

Thus remains the case with our concepts as with the laws of social history.

Marx and Engels have set us a glorious example on how to deepen our understanding of the laws of social development according to changes in reality. They constantly revised and enriched their understanding of the laws of the capitalistic development according to the dynamic changes and manifestations of capitalism, to overcome the historical limitations in their understanding. In the mid-1840s, Marx and Engels decided that the capitalist society will be replaced by the communist society. They revealed the objective law that capitalism is bound to perish and socialism is bound to win, as seen in many of their works, including *The German Ideology* co-authored in 1845–1846, *The Poverty of Philosophy* published in July, 1847, and *The Communist Manifesto* published in February, 1848. During the European Revolutions of 1848, they thought that the proletariat should not stop at the phase of the bourgeois democratic revolution. Instead, the proletariat should continue their revolution and eliminate the capitalist system with a coup de grâce. In his letter to Engels on June 7, 1849, not long after the failure of the 1948 revolution, Marx predicted that another revolution would soon break out. He said, "The volcanic eruption of revolution has never been as imminent as in today's Paris."[34] He changed his view, however, after seeing the general economic prosperity in 1850 all across Europe. He thought,

> There is no real revolution in a generally prosperous situation, which is the productivity in a bourgeoisie society is developing at a full speed that this society can reach. *A revolution is possible only when* the two elements, namely *modern productivity and bourgeoisie production mode, are in contradiction.*[35]

In 1857, a world-wide financial crisis broke out and Marx held the expectation that a proletariat revolution could eliminate capitalism once and for all. However, the crisis did not lead to the end of capitalism, which continued to develop. Hence, Marx put forth his famous argument of "two 'definitely not'" in his 1859 work of *A Contribution to the Critique of Political Economy*,

> No matter what social form it is, it will definitely not die before its full capacity of productivity is leveraged; the newer and higher production relation will definitely not appear before its material conditions for existence matures in the old society.[36]

In spite of this, Marx still held the idea that it would not be too long before the end of capitalism, as evidenced by his reclaimed statement in the first volume of *Capital* published in 1867, that "the knell of capitalist private property sounds. The expropriators are expropriated."[37] After the failed attempt of the Paris Commune, capitalism once again entered a new era when it enjoyed a relatively stable political environment and a flourishing economy in the 1870s. Marx and Engels came to further realize that the productivity back then was not developed to the point that would terminate capitalism. Marx, in his letter to N F Danielson on April 10, 1879, discussing the serious 1873 worldwide economic crisis, said,

> regardless the possible trends of the development of this crisis—take a careful observation on the crisis, it is of course vitally important for the researcher and professional theorist on capitalist production—, it will pass just like previous crisis and usher in a new "industrial cycle" featuring all kinds of different phases like prosperity.

We know that it was quite a serious economic crisis with a global impact. But back then, Marx had already realized that even an economic crisis so severe was not powerful enough to kill capitalism, which continued its normal course after the crisis. It was based on this understanding that Marx made a mockery of "the extremely desperate emotions of the lazy people in the British commercial and industrial circles."[38] Engels, before his death, wrote the introduction for Marx's book *The Class Struggles in France, 1848 to 1850.* Engels wrote that capitalism still had a powerful ability to expand and the economic development of Europe was far from mature enough to eradicate the production mode of capitalism. Engels also publicly admitted that the idea he and Marx had put forward in 1848 and 1871—to attempt to win a socialist revolution with one sudden sweeping attack—had been "wrong" and "a mist," "a vision" thus "incorrect" and "fruitless" so that it had been "impossible to achieve."[39] It is their earnest scientific attitude and arduous exploration that enabled Marx and Engel to overcome the historical limitations of their understanding and to gradually acquire a complete comprehension of the development laws of capitalism. Therefore, they have "respected the objective laws" and "acted in accordance with the objective laws" in their formulation of the fighting strategies for the proletariat.

It has been over a hundred years since Marx and Engels passed away. During this time, many new changes have taken place in capitalism. Despite multiple economic crises and recessions, capitalism generally has greatly developed. After World War II especially, mostly stable development remained for a long time. Capitalism is still predominant around the world, signaling no foreseeable death. Marx and Engels' underestimation of the life of capitalism in a certain historical period is indeed contrary to the intrinsic history of capitalism. However, it is undoubtedly wrong to conclude that Marxism is "out of date." This conclusion fails to comprehend the intrinsic logic of the historical changes seen in Marx and Engels' idea regarding the life of capitalism. It also fails to comprehend the profound analysis of the natural features of capitalism and the revelation of the law that capitalism is destined to perish. It can be explicitly drawn from the brief review of the historical changes in Marx and Engels' ideas on the life of capitalism as compared with the objective historical course of capitalism that the intrinsic logic of the historical changes of their ideas remains aligned and synchronized with the general trend. The historical course of capitalism after the deaths of Marx and Engels is not a falsification but verification of their ideas regarding the life of capitalism. It needs further emphasis that despite the fact that Engels admitted the vitality and expanding capabilities of capitalism in his time, what he stressed more than anything was that the demise of capitalism is inevitable and irreversible.

Notes

1 *An Anthology of Marx and Engels* (Vol. 4). (2009). Beijing, China: People's Publishing House, 301–302.
2 Zhao Jiaxiang et al. (1999). *A Course in Historical Materialism.* Beijing, China: Peking University Press, 461–462.

3 Zhao Jiaxiang et al. (2003). *A Course in Marxist Philosophy.* Beijing, China: Peking University Press, 448.
4 *An Anthology of Marx and Engels* (Vol. 5). (2009). Beijing, China: People's Publishing House, 429.
5 Huang Nansen & Yang Shoukan. (1993). *The New Dictionary of Philosophy.* Taiyuan, China: Shanxi Education Press, 132.
6 Giambattista Vico. (1989). *New Science* (Zhu Guangqian, Trans.). Beijing, China: The Commercial Press, 160, 162.
7 Immanuel Kant. (1990). *Critique of Historical Reason* (He Zhaowu, Trans.). Beijing, China: The Commercial Press, 2.
8 G. W. F. Hegel. (1980). *The Shorter Logic* (He Lin, Trans.). Beijing, China: The Commercial Press, 394–395. Emphasis added.
9 *Collected Works of Marx and Engels* (Vol. 3). (2002). Beijing, China: People's Publishing House, 520.
10 *Collected Works of Marx and Engels* (Vol. 2). (1957). Beijing, China: People's Publishing House, 100–101. Emphasis added.
11 *Collected Works of Marx and Engels* (Vol. 2). (1957). Beijing, China: People's Publishing House, 108. Emphasis added.
12 *Collected Works of Marx and Engels* (Vol. 2). (1957). Beijing, China: People's Publishing House, 118–119. Emphasis added.
13 *An Anthology of Marx and Engels* (Vol. 10). (2009). Beijing, China: People's Publishing House, 44.
14 *An Anthology of Marx and Engels* (Vol. 9). (2009). Beijing, China: People's Publishing House, 413.
15 *An Anthology of Marx and Engels* (Vol. 5). (2009). Beijing, China: People's Publishing House, 208.
16 *An Anthology of Marx and Engels* (Vol. 4). (2009). Beijing, China: People's Publishing House, 302–303.
17 *An Anthology of Marx and Engels* (Vol. 10). (2009). Beijing, China: People's Publishing House, 592–593.
18 *An Anthology of Marx and Engels* (Vol. 10). (2009). Beijing, China: People's Publishing House, 559–560.
19 *An Anthology of Marx and Engels* (Vol. 10). (2009). Beijing, China: People's Publishing House, 560.
20 *An Anthology of Marx and Engels* (Vol. 9). (2009). Beijing, China: People's Publishing House, 494.
21 *An Anthology of Marx and Engels* (Vol. 9). (2009). Beijing, China: People's Publishing House, 91.
22 *An Anthology of Marx and Engels* (Vol. 5). (2009). Beijing, China: People's Publishing House, 10.
23 *An Anthology of Marx and Engels* (Vol. 9). (2009). Beijing, China: People's Publishing House, 21–22.
24 *An Anthology of Marx and Engels* (Vol. 5). (2009). Beijing, China: People's Publishing House, 21.
25 *An Anthology of Marx and Engels* (Vol. 10). (2009). Beijing, China: People's Publishing House, 225.
26 *Collected Works of Marx and Engels* (Vol. 21). (2003). Beijing, China: People's Publishing House, 306.
27 *An Anthology of Marx and Engels* (Vol. 10). (2009). Beijing, China: People's Publishing House, 593–694.
28 *An Anthology of Marx and Engels* (Vol. 7). (2009). Beijing, China: People's Publishing House, 181.
29 *An Anthology of Marx and Engels* (Vol. 10). (2009). Beijing, China: People's Publishing House, 693.

30 Popper, K. (1987). *The Poverty of Historicism* (Du Ruji & Qiu Renzong, Trans.). Beijing, China: Huaxia Press, 91.
31 Popper, K. (1987). *The Poverty of Historicism* (Du Ruji & Qiu Renzong, Trans.). Beijing, China: Huaxia Press, 81.
32 *An Anthology of Marx and Engels* (Vol. 5). (2009). Beijing, China: People's Publishing House, 8.
33 *An Anthology of Marx and Engels* (Vol. 7). (2009). Beijing, China: People's Publishing House, 17.
34 *Collected Works of Marx and Engels* (Vol. 27). (1972). Beijing, China: People's Publishing House, 154.
35 *An Anthology of Marx and Engels* (Vol. 2). (2009). Beijing, China: People's Publishing House, 196. Emphasis added.
36 *An Anthology of Marx and Engels* (Vol. 2). (2009). Beijing, China: People's Publishing House, 592.
37 *An Anthology of Marx and Engels* (Vol. 5). (2009). Beijing, China: People's Publishing House, 874.
38 *An Anthology of Marx and Engels* (Vol. 10). (2009). Beijing, China: People's Publishing House, 433, 431.
39 *An Anthology of Marx and Engels* (Vol. 4). (2009). Beijing, China: People's Publishing House, 538–542.

3 Historical determinism, subjective choice, and their relations

Historical determinism, subjective choice, and the relations between the two are important issues in historical studies. Great controversy among scholars exists over these issues. This chapter focuses on such controversy in the hope to elicit more discussion from my scholarly peers.

3.1 The classification of historical philosophy and the theoretical origins of historical nondeterminism

Historical determinism and historical nondeterminism oppose each other in their understanding of historical development. We will first explore the theoretical origins of historical nondeterminism. We will begin our exploration by defining historical philosophy and its classification. Before that, we need to first define "history." Generally, "history" may have two definitions. One, history refers to human activities and products (past, present, and future) and human plans for the future. Two, history refers to the narration and interpretation of human activities and products (past, present, and future) and human plans for the future. For our purpose, we will use "history" for the first definition, and "historical interpretation" for the second definition.

In Western English-speaking countries, there is a duality in historical philosophy, again based on two different definitions of "history." This duality was first proposed by the British historical philosopher Walsh in *Philosophy of History: An Introduction* published in 1951. Walsh calls the study of the historical process itself the "speculative philosophy of history," and the interpretation of history as the "critical philosophy of history." In German-speaking countries, however, the two terms that straddle our duality are respectively "material philosophy of history" and "formalistic philosophy of history." In the vocabulary of Chinese scholars, the two terms are, respectively, "metaphysics of history"/"the philosophy of history"/"ontological history" on the one hand, and on the other, "historiographic epistemology"/"historiographic philosophy"/"philosophy of historical epistemology."[1]

It should be noted that, in philosophy of history, the term "history" encompasses the past, the present, and the future along the dimension of time. For example, almost all studies of philosophy of history cover human destiny and historical trends. Hence, the past, the present, and the future all need to be involved. As another example, when we say that someone will change history through a certain feat, it will inevitably involve that person's present and future. The past, the present, and the future compose an integrated trinity of time. The past evolves to become the present, which in turn evolves to become the future, all determined by the intrinsic dynamics and contradictions within the historical process. To understand human history correctly, we must consider the integrated trinity of time. The study of the philosophy of history reviews the past, guides the present, and plans for a better future.

According to research by Max Nordau, a French scholar, the term "philosophy of history" was first used by the French thinker Jean Bodin in 1650, and then by Voltaire in 1765. However, neither of them had built a systematic philosophy of history. Italian historical philosopher Battista Vico is generally considered the founder of the discipline of philosophy of history. His book *New Science* (full name: *Principles of New Science about the Common Nature of Nations*) published in 1725 inaugurated the Western philosophy of history. However, at Vico's time, philosophy of history had not yet been recognized as a discipline. That recognition did not come until two publications: The first part of *Reflections on the Philosophy of the History of Mankind* by German historical philosopher Johann Gottfried Herder in 1784, and Hegel's *Lectures on the Philosophy of History* published posthumously in 1837.[2]

Since the establishment of the philosophy of history between early 18th and late 19th centuries, Western historical philosophers devoted themselves to exploring the question on historical ontology—the essence of the historical process. Therefore, this period may be called the stage of ontology in the philosophy of history. Herbert Bradley, a British neo-Hegelian, published *The Presuppositions of Critical History* in 1874, which marked the historical philosophy's turn toward epistemology. Bradley's work explored how historical understanding becomes possible. The work systematically discussed the possibility of reaching an objective understanding of history. As a result, many Western historical philosophers regard Bradley as one of the founders of critical historical philosophy (or "historical epistemology" as known today).

From the late 1800s to late 1930s, Western philosophy of history transitioned to epistemology. Many historical philosophers at this time combined investigation of historical ontology with that of historical epistemology. The year 1938 saw two publications in the field: *Introduction to the Philosophy of History* by Raymond Aron, a French historian, and *The Problem of Historical Knowledge: An Answer to Relativism* by American historical philosopher Maurice Mandelbaum. These publications officially inaugurated historical epistemology as an independent discipline. In 1951, Walsh named the discipline "Critical Philosophy of History." Speculative philosophy of history has a history of over 200 years, and has long dominated the modern Western philosophy of history. Speculative historical philosophers, such as Vico, Fourier, Kant, Hegel, Comte, Spengler, Toynbee, and Jaspers, all advocated historical determinism. However, from late 1800s, speculative philosophy of history began to diminish, while critical philosophy of history flourished from a subsidiary into a leader in historical studies. Voltaire, Windelband, Rickert, Bradley, Croce, Collingwood, and many other critical historical philosophers doubted, denied, and criticized historical determinism, especially that by Marx. The negation and criticism of historical determinism in Chinese academia generally follow the influence of Western critical historical philosophers.

Some Chinese scholars dichotomize between historical determinism and the human possibility to change the world. They believe that Marxist philosophy is only about changing the world, and that Marxist philosophy affirms the human capability to change world history—an idea that presupposes the changeability of the world. That is, history is not a predetermined immutability (historical determinism is sometimes interpreted as "pure predetermination." This represents a misinterpretation of historical determinism as intended by historical materialism. This will be analyzed in detail below). If we accept Marx's historical materialism as a kind of historical determinism, it may seem logically impossible and incomprehensible for humankind to change the world. That is, we now face the argument that historical determinism contradicts the concepts of the world's changeability and subjective choice. Therefore, the argument goes, historical determinism is wrong; historical materialism can only be historical nondeterminism rather than historical determinism. But I will have to disagree and demonstrate below that the above argument is not appropriately formulated.

3.2   The determinism of historical materialism

To those scholars who believe that the possibility to change the world contradicts historical determinism, the fundamental question is whether or not historical materialism stands for historical determinism. Regrettably, these scholars neither seem to have answered nor even heeded this question. They seem to equate historical materialism with historical determinism, or consider historical materialism as historical nondeterminism and take it as a self-evident theoretical premise. This is rather curious. I would argue that Marx and Engels's historical materialism is historical determinism rather than historical nondeterminism. This is a basic and even evident viewpoint of historical materialism. So, in some sense, it does not seem hard to take historical materialism as the theoretical premise of historical determinism. Many Chinese scholars, however, seem to deny this theoretical premise. Therefore, we need to offer additional discussion here even if such discussion may appear cliché.

The determinism of historical materialism acknowledges the objective regularity, necessity, and causality in social development. It believes that human history is a natural process. The opposite of historical determinism is historical nondeterminism. Historical nondeterminism denies human history as a natural process, wherein there is no causality, regularity, and necessity. Historical determinism permeates representative works of classical Marxist writers. A brief survey follows.

The German Ideology composed by Marx and Engels in 1845 and 1846, which symbolized the formation of historical materialism, systematically expounds historical determinism.

First of all, it contends that social existence determines social consciousness. When criticizing historical idealism, which holds that consciousness determines existence, as young Hegelians such as Bruno Bauer believed, Marx and Engels pointed out, "Life is not determined by consciousness, but consciousness by life."[3] The materialist conception of history differs from the idealist conception of history.

> [The materialist conception] has not ... in every period [looked] for a category, but remains constantly on the real ground of history; it does not explain practice from the idea but explains the formation of ideas from material practice.[4]

Second, historical materialism demonstrates the interaction between human and the environment. Marx and Engels said,

> At each stage there is found a material result: a sum of productive forces, an historically created relation of individuals to nature and to one another, which is handed down to each generation from its predecessor; a mass of productive forces, capital funds and conditions, which, on the one hand, is indeed modified by the new generation, but also on the other prescribes for it its conditions of life and gives it a definite development, a special character. It shows that circumstances make men just as much as men make circumstances.[5]

"Circumstances make men" argues for historical determinism—that humans' ability to create history is restrained by the environment. "Men make circumstances" argues for the subjective choice and historical dialectics. The unity between "circumstances make men" and "men make circumstances" parallels the unity between historical determinism and subjective choice.

Third, historical materialism holds that social reforms must be based on necessary material and human conditions. To Marx and Engels, material living conditions of different ages determine

> whether or not the periodically recurring revolutionary convulsion will be strong enough to overthrow the basis of the entire existing system. And if these material elements of a complete revolution are not present (namely, on the one hand the existing productive forces, on the other the formation of a revolutionary mass, which revolts not only against separate conditions of society up till then, but against the very "production of life" till then, the "total activity" on which it was based), then, as far as practical development is concerned, it is absolutely immaterial whether the idea of this revolution has been expressed a hundred times already, as the history of communism proves.[6]

Finally, historical materialism holds that productive forces determine the form of communication and the economic base determines the superstructure. It also addresses the law of the evolution of social forms. To Marx and Engels, the contradiction between productive forces and forms of communication is fundamental in human society. All conflicts are rooted in this fundamental contradiction. The increasing severity of this contradiction will inevitably lead to revolution. The civil society that grows out of production and communication constitutes the foundation of nations and the superstructure of their ideology. The contradiction between productive forces and forms of communication creates the iterative interactions among various forms of communication.

> In the place of an earlier form of intercourse, which has become a fetter, a new one is put, corresponding to the more developed productive forces and, hence, to the advanced mode of the self-activity of individuals—a form which in its turn becomes a fetter and is then replaced by another. Since these conditions correspond at every stage to the simultaneous development of the productive forces, their history is at the same time the history of the evolving productive forces taken over by each new generation, and is, therefore, the history of the development of the forces of the individuals themselves.[7]

Marx and Engels then believed that human history in turn experienced five successive ownership forms, namely tribal ownership, ancient communal and state ownership, feudal ownership or estate property, capitalistic ownership, and communistic ownership. Based on these five forms of ownership, five social forms emerge in succession, namely the tribal ownership society, slave society, feudalistic society, capitalistic society, and communistic society.

Social existence determines social consciousness; the environment determines men and vice versa; the productive forces determine the form of communication; the economic base determines the superstructure; and social revolution and successive replacement of social forms emerges on a necessary material and human base. These above arguments of historical materialism give the fundamentals of historical determinism.

In his letter to Pavel Annenkov on December 28, 1846, Marx brilliantly discussed historical determinism. According to Marx, productive forces are the foundation of the entire human history. People are not free to choose their productive forces, which are products of previous activities controlled by those in power. The subsequent generation receives the productive forces from the previous generation, which constitute the material condition for the new production process. Production forces thus link together and create human history. With the development of productive forces and social relations, history becomes that of humans. Material relations constitute the foundation of all human relations. Material relations are the basis upon which material and social activities operate. Every social form is the product of interpersonal interaction. However, are humans free to choose their social form? Marx says,

By no means. If you assume a given state of development of man's productive faculties, you will have a corresponding form of commerce and consumption. If you assume given stages of development in production, commerce or consumption, you will have a corresponding form of social constitution, a corresponding organisation, whether of the family, of the estates or of the classes—in a word, a corresponding civil society. If you assume this or that civil society, you will have this or that political system, which is but the official expression of civil society.[8]

In *The Poverty of Philosophy* published in July 1847, Marx made it clearer,

Social relations are closely bound up with productive forces. In acquiring new productive forces men change their mode of production; and in changing their mode of production, in changing the way of earning their living, they change all their social relations. The hand-mill gives you society with the feudal lord; the steam-mill, society with the industrial capitalist.[9]

Here, without explicit use of the term "historical determinism," Marx offered a convincing demonstration of it. First, people cannot freely choose the productive forces and production relations (e.g., forms of production, of exchange, and of consumption). Neither can they choose their own social forms. The reason is, when people begin their social life, they always fall heir to pre-existing productive forces, production relations, and social forms passed down from their predecessors. All these factors combine to determine human life and activities. Second, people cannot freely determine—although they are able to modify—the productive forces, production relations, and their social form. Furthermore, they will not foretell the resultant of their activities as determined by the above list of factors, despite the fact that their activities are motivated by their own purpose and needs. Their wishes and purposes may be realized partially or not at all. Sometimes, the result of their activities may turn out to oppose what they desire. Why? Because the result of human activities is determined by a large complexity of inter-dynamic forces unpredictable to the individual.

In his preface to *A Contribution to the Critique of Political Economy* published in 1859, Marx offered a comprehensive discussion of historical determinism. He said, productive forces determine production relations; the economic foundation determines the superstructure; the mode of production constrains entire social life; social existence determines social consciousness; and successive revolutions and replacements of social forms find their root in material conditions.[10]

In the preface to *Capital Volume I* published in 1867, Marx discussed the idea that the development of social history is a natural process. He said:

I paint the capitalist and the landlord in no sense couleur de rose [i.e., seen through rose-tinted glasses]. But here individuals are dealt with only in so far as they are the personifications of economic categories, embodiments of particular class-relations and class-interests. My standpoint, from which the evolution of the economic formation of society is viewed as a process of natural history, can less than any other make the individual responsible for relations whose creature he socially remains, however much he may subjectively raise himself above them.[11]

The economic formation of society could be viewed as a process of natural history. As with nature, it is an objective, material, and dialectical process, a process of objective regularity independent of human will. People cannot subjectively cancel the objective law of social development or any stage of it. As Marx put it:

And even when a society has got upon the right track for the discovery of the natural laws of its movement—and it is the ultimate aim of this work, to lay bare the economic law of motion of modern society—it can neither clear by bold leaps, nor remove by legal enactments, the obstacles offered by the successive phases of its normal development. But it can shorten and lessen the birth-pangs.[12]

Marx affirmed as well as qualified the significant role of humans' practical activities in history's development. Human activities can only alleviate their own suffering in social development or shorten the course of social development, and such activities are restricted by the objective regularity of social development. People cannot subjectively and arbitrarily cancel any stage of social development.

Ludwig Feuerbach and the End of Classical German Philosophy by Engels in 1886 comprehensively and thoroughly discusses the objective regularity of historical development. The book offers a full and deep argument for historical determinism. Before the emergence of historical materialism, historical idealism dominated the world. Historical idealism used delusional interconnections in the mind to replace actual interconnections intrinsic in history itself, held that history was dominated by the subjective ideas or ideological motives of great men, and denied that historical development has objective regularity impervious to humans' subjective will. To eliminate the nefarious influence of idealism in the realm of history, Engels contended:

Here, therefore, just as in the realm of nature, it was necessary to do away with these fabricated, artificial interconnections by the discovery of the real ones—a task which ultimately amounts to the discovery of the general laws of motion which assert themselves as the ruling ones in the history of human society.[13]

Engels elaborated the relations between the objective regularity of historical development and the practical activities of humans (the historical subject) by differentiating between the laws of social history and natural laws. An important difference is that changes in nature are blind and unconscious. The law of nature shows itself blindly and unconsciously. Human activities, however, are conscious and purposeful, and come to shape human history and society. Humans fashion their own history through practical activities, out of which arise the laws of history's evolution. Moreover, the law of human society and history can materialize not spontaneously but through conscious and purposeful human activities, without which no human history occurs, let alone the law thereof.

Engels held that the difference between historical materialism and historical idealism lies not in their recognition of the role of conscious and purposeful human activities in the historical process, nor in their recognition of the role of the spiritual power (human will), but in whether considering the spiritual power or the material power as the primal driver behind history's development. History is indeed a product of the intricate interactions among a host of individual forces. Historical idealism is premised on people's ideological motives which it regards as the most fundamental driving force behind history. Historical materialism, on the other hand, lays bare a deeper driving force behind humans' ideological motivations. As Engels said, historical idealism

> takes the ideal driving forces which operate there as ultimate causes, instead of investigating what is behind them, what are the driving forces of these driving forces. This inconsistency does not lie in the fact that *ideal* driving forces are recognized, but in the investigation not being carried further back behind these into their motive causes.[14]

So, how do we find the driving force and motivation behind the ideal and spiritual forces? Engels believed that the most fundamental method is to attribute personal activities to class activities and mass activities. He said:

> When, therefore, it is a question of investigating the driving powers which ... lie behind the motives of men who act in history and which constitute the real ultimate driving forces of history, then it is not a question so much of the motives of single individuals, however eminent, as of those motives which set in motion great masses, whole people, and again whole classes of the people in each people; and this, too, not merely for an instant, like the transient flaring up of a straw-fire which quickly dies down, but as a lasting action resulting in a great historical transformation. To ascertain the driving causes which here in the minds of acting masses and their leaders—the so-called great men—are reflected as conscious motives, clearly or unclearly, directly or in an ideological, even glorified, form—is the only path which can put us on the track of the laws holding sway both in history as a whole, and at particular periods and in particular lands.[15]

Engels then pointed out that before the capitalist society, the connection between the ideological motives of historical figures and the driving power behind was confusing and hidden. It was almost impossible to discover it at that time. In the capitalist society, this connection became simple, making it possible for people to discover the motivation behind ideological motives. The history of England and France fully shows that the struggle of the bourgeoisie against the feudal aristocracy and the proletariat against the bourgeoisie serves as the driving force of the modern history for these two advanced countries. How did these classes come about? It is due to economic reasons and certain production methods. All classes are in different positions in production relations and have different interests, and, therefore, they struggle with each other in various forms. This shows that the driving forces behind ideological motives are the production method of life's materials.

Acknowledging the role of individuals and their ideological motives in history also means acknowledging the role of accident in history. This is because the personality, hobbies, habits, knowledge level, physical conditions, and experiences of individuals all have a certain degree of accident; people's ideological motives are ultimately rooted in material matters, though they are also partially affected by accidental factors operative in social development. The difference between historical materialism and historical idealism is whether recognition is given to the existence of accident and its role in history. Historical idealism attributes the development of history completely to accident, while historical materialism detects hidden necessity (i.e., objective regularity) behind accident. In the realm of history, "[f]or here, also, on the whole, in spite of the consciously desired aims of all individuals, accident apparently reigns on the surface." "But where on the surface accident holds sway, there actually it is always governed by inner hidden laws, and it is only a matter of discovering these laws."[16]

Our investigation above makes it now easier to conclude that the historical materialism of Marx and Engels supports historical determinism rather than historical nondeterminism.

3.3 The determinism of historical materialism is materialistic and dialectical

To illustrate that historical determinism is not antithetical to the possibility of changing the world, it is necessary not only to affirm that historical materialism is a historical determinism, but also to explain what kind of determinism is the determinism of historical materialism.

Determinism is a complex multifaceted concept. In terms of the basic nature of philosophy, there is a determinism of materialism and a determinism of idealism; from the perspective of existence, there is a natural determinism and a historical determinism; from the perspective of the forms of science, there is a strict determinism and a statistical determinism (or univocal determinism and probabilistic determinism); from the forms of history, there is an ancient naive determinism, a medieval theological determinism, a modern mechanical determinism, and Hegel's idealistic and dialectical determinism, and a Marxist materialistic and dialectical determinism (many scholars in China have labeled the materialistic and dialectical determinism as system determinism in recent years). The historical determinism of historical materialism is a materialistic and dialectical determinism. There are many existing studies and discussions in China on various forms of determinism, so no further discussion on them will be offered here. Only the dialectical materialist determinism of historical materialism will be discussed here. As already mentioned, the determinism of historical materialism is a theory that recognizes that the development of society has objective regularity, necessity, and causal constraints. It is a determinism based on materialism and dialectics, unlike the mechanical determinism and the determinism of idealism. In fact, the determinism of historical materialism believes that the development of society has an objective regularity impervious to the subjective will of men. This determinism also opposes the historical fatalism and historical pre-formationism that people are powerless in the face of objective laws. It is an agency determinism based on the practical activities of men as the subjects of history. The determinism of historical materialism does not deny or reject the role of humans' active and history-making activities, and even considers them as the premise for historical determinism. If the determinism of historical materialism loses this premise, the practical activities of men as the subjects of history cannot be carried out. Judging from the determinism of historical materialism, the understanding and revealing of the objective regularity of the development of history open up a vast world for exploring the history-making and active activities of men as the subjects of history, so that human agency can enjoy more freedom and employ initiative, thus creating history with greater consciousness and compliance with objective laws.

In order to illustrate that the determinism of historical materialism is dialectical and materialistic, it is necessary to illustrate that historical determinism and the possibility of changing the world are not contradictory to but interconnected with each other. Several issues await clarification here: First, the relation between historical determinism and human agency; second, the relation between univocal determinism and probabilistic determinism; third, the relation between historical determinism and subjective choice; fourth, the relation between freedom and necessity. Each receives its discussion below.

3.3.1 The relationship between historical determinism and human agency

The relationship between historical determinism and human agency is, in fact, the relationship between historical determinism and humans' practical activities that change the world. The founders of historical materialism and their successors have provided many insightful and profound discussions on this topic.

In *The Eighteenth Brumaire of Louis Bonaparte*, Marx said, "Men make their own history, but they do not make it as they please; they do not make it under self-selected circumstances, but under circumstances existing already, given and transmitted from the past."[17] By "men make their own history," Marx recognized that men, the subjects of history, have the capability of making and changing history via practical activities. Believing that men "do not make history as they please," and "they do not make it under self-selected circumstances," "but under circumstances existing already, given and transmitted from the past," Marx recognized that the development of history has objective regularity, necessity, and causal constraints, and that humans' history-making activities are restricted by established historical conditions and objective laws. In short, Marx recognized historical determinism. While some scholars believe that Marx's statement means that although this kind of creation and change of the world is conditional and constrained, and it is only a change within the existing world, and does not come out of thin air, yet history is made by men, rather than developing itself by making men its tools. This explanation is ambiguous and only recognizes that men themselves create their own history and refrains from talking about the historical determinism contained in this sentence.

When talking about the relationship between humans and history in *The Poverty of Philosophy*, Marx believed that men themselves are both the "authors of the history" and "the actors of their own drama."[18] "Men are the authors of the history" means that history is created by practical activities of humans, and humans can create history, change history, and change the world. "Men are the actors of their own drama" means that men are constrained by the history they have made and by the objective laws therein. To recognize that men are constrained by history and its objective laws is to recognize historical determinism. Marx's metaphor that men are both "authors" and "actors of drama" vividly and profoundly explains the relationship between historical determinism and human agency. Engels mentioned in *Anti-Dühring* that historical laws are "the laws of his own social action,"[19] which expresses the same idea as Marx's metaphor mentioned above.

In *What the "Friends of the People" Are and How They Fight the Social-Democrats?*, Lenin criticized the wrong viewpoints of a Russian subjective sociologist Mikhailovsky, who counterposed historical necessity and human activities. Lenin offered a profound discussion of the dialectical relationship between historical determinism and subjective agency. Mikhailovsky talked about "the conflict between the idea of historical necessity and the significance of individual activities," called himself a sociologist, and believed that socially active figures are "activated marionettes, manipulated from a mysterious underground by the immanent laws of historical necessity." Lenin thought that this was one of the favorite topics of Mikhailovsky, namely, the conflict between determinism and morality, between historical necessity and the significance of the individual. Mikhailovsky uttered an infinite amount of sentimental, philistine nonsense in order to settle this conflict in favor of morality and the role of the individual. Actually, there is no conflict here at all; it has been invented by Mr. Mikhailovsky, who feared (not without reason) that determinism would cut the ground from under the philistine morality he loved so dearly. Lenin said:

> The idea of determinism, which postulates that human acts are necessitated and rejects the absurd tale about free will, in no way destroys man's reason or conscience, or appraisal of his actions. Quite the contrary, only the determinist view makes a strict and correct appraisal possible instead of attributing everything you please to free will. Similarly, the idea of historical necessity does not in the least undermine the role of the individual in history: all history is made up of the actions of individuals, who are undoubtedly active figures.[20]

Lenin's argument insightfully illustrates the congruence among historical determinism, historical necessity, and human agency, and that historical determinism is the objective basis for the appraisal of human reason, morality, conscience, and actions.

Mao Zedong developed the thoughts of Marx, Engels, and Lenin. In his *On Protracted War*, taking the Anti-Japanese War as an example, Mao vividly and profoundly explained the relationship between respecting objective laws and giving full play to people's subjective initiative. He stated:

> In seeking victory, those who direct a war cannot overstep the limitations imposed by the objective conditions; within these limitations, however, they can and must play a dynamic role in striving for victory. The stage of action for commanders in a war must be built upon objective possibilities, but on that stage they can direct the performance of many a drama, full of sound and color, power and grandeur.

We do not want any of our commanders in the war to detach himself from the objective conditions and become a blundering hothead, but we decidedly want every commander to become a general who is both bold and sagacious. Our commanders should have not only the boldness to overwhelm the enemy but also the ability to remain masters of the situation throughout the changes and vicissitudes of the entire war. Swimming in the ocean of war, they must not flounder but make sure of reaching the opposite shore with measured strokes. Strategy and tactics, as the laws for directing war, constitute the art of swimming in the ocean of war.[21]

Here, Mao Zedong elucidated the relation between historical determinism and active human agency.

3.3.2 The relationship between univocal and probabilistic determinism

Correctly understanding the relationship between univocal and probabilistic determinism helps in interpreting the internal unity between historical determinism and the possibility of people changing the world through practical activities.

Univocal determinism is a definite relation between nature and things in human society. The so-called definite relation means that the existence and occurrence of one thing *inevitably* lead to that of another. On the contrary, if the existence and occurrence of one thing *may* lead to that of another, then the relationship between these two things is a non-definite relation. Unlike univocal determinism, probabilistic determinism addresses the *degree of probability* of things or phenomena in nature and human society. If there exists a high degree of occurrence or large number of occurrences, the relationship among things and phenomena is definite; otherwise, non-definite. Probabilistic determinism belongs to the realm of statistical laws.

Univocal and probabilistic determinisms have different research objects and scopes of application. Univocal determinism takes the individual as research object. Within the investigation scope of univocal determinism, the investigation of an aggregate of individuals and one individual are equivalent. Therefore, by studying the nature and regularity of individuals, it is possible to understand the character and regularity of the aggregate, and the character and regularity of the individual are representative of the aggregate. Probabilistic determinism takes the aggregate as its investigation object. Within the investigation scope of probabilistic determinism, the individual and the aggregate of individuals are not equivalent, but have different characters and laws of development. Due to varied constraints and influences, the movement of each individual is highly contingent, with no established rules to follow. Only by investigating the sum (aggregate) of individuals, can we employ statistical laws to find out, to a certain degree, the regularity of the individual, which is then applied to derive the inevitable features of a large number of occasional and random phenomena.

Human society is a complex macro-system. In it, there are interactions among economic, political, ideological, and cultural factors, as well as cooperation and conflicts among individuals, groups, classes, and people. Every historical event is constrained and influenced by an infinite number of social factors. Therefore, it is difficult to precisely determine the course of historical events. Moreover, the interaction between these factors and their historical results cannot be described via univocal determinism, but via statistical laws. Essentially, social laws follow the probabilistic determinism.

Does the interpretation of social laws completely exclude univocal determinism? No. In order to study the internal structure of a certain social factor and the interaction of various internal factors, we can extract this social factor from its connection with other factors for investigation, and temporarily put aside its interrelation with other factors. For example, in order to study the relationship between productive forces and relations of production, we can isolate material production from factors in the social macro-system, and temporarily put aside other factors' influence on the development of production. Therefore, we can conclude that relations of production must be adapted to the character of productive forces. Under this circumstance, univocal determinism can and must be adopted. However, when factors that restrict social production are investigated all around, the relationship between productive forces and relations of production should be put into its connection with other factors, and it is the time when the probabilistic determinism shall be employed. Investigated from the perspective of the univocal determinism, the relationship between productive forces and relations of production bears definiteness, while from the perspective of probabilistic determinism, it is relative, rather than absolute. Therefore, univocal and probabilistic determinism play different roles in interpreting the objectivity of social laws, and they should be employed in combination. Investigated from the perspective of their combination, the relationship between productive forces and relations of production is the unity of certainty and uncertainty, i.e., the relationship bears both certainty and uncertainty. If we interpret social laws only using univocal determinism, we will certainly fall into mechanical determinism and fatalism. If we completely exclude the univocal determinism, or use the probabilistic determinism only, we will violate the materialist view of historical development. Therefore, it will be impossible to reach the conclusion that the development of social history has inevitability and objective regularity.

The relationship between linear and nonlinear interactions is similar to that between univocal and probabilistic determinism. Modern science and philosophy generally classify complex interactions into linear and nonlinear interactions. Linear interactions refer to the interactions that can be described by linear equations (the relation between zero power and first power) and linear differential equations (whose solutions can be linearly superposed), such as the relationship between action and reaction force, the relationship between action force and the rate of change of momentum in mechanics, the relationship between density gradient and mass diffusion in thermodynamics, and the relationship between the induced emf and the change in magnetic flux in electricity, etc. These are all linear interactions. In the past, people paid much attention to linear interactions and held that no matter how complex interactions are, they could be regarded as linear processes or a simple superposition of linear processes. Since the 20th century, with the development of science, people have tried to comprehensively understand the evolution of a complex material system composed of multiple factors and processes, and the complex contents of interactions have been increasingly exposed. It is generally seen that the interaction between various elements and processes in the vast majority of material systems is difficult to describe using linear equations. Therefore, the study of nonlinear interactions is necessary. The so-called nonlinear interaction means that the mathematical equation describing the interaction contains at least one nonlinear term (multiple terms). Due to the inclusion of nonlinear terms, the solution to this mathematical equation is not unique. The interpretation of human history should employ concepts and methods of nonlinear interaction, while the interpretation of each factor and link in human history should employ concepts and methods of linear interaction. In the history of human society as in nature, nonlinear interactions encompass rather than negate linear interactions. Interpreting history only with linear interactions will oversimplify the intrinsic complexity of history. Consequently, historical development is given one possibility; the diversity in historical development is negated. The exclusion of linear interactions in historical interpretations will negate the certainty of historical development, leading to historical relativism and the negation of the necessity and objective regularity in historical development.

3.3.3 *Relationship between historical determinism and subjective choice*

Subjective choice is an activity in which, based on the cognition of historical contradictions and their development trends, people, as the historical subject, determine the way, directions, goals, and methods of their behaviors that proceed from their own goals, needs, aspirations, knowledge structure, experience, and skills. Recognizing the changeability of the world and social history, we must not only adhere to historical determinism, but also affirm the role of subjective choice and organically combine the two. Recognizing historical determinism is the premise and basis for affirming the role of subjective choice;

affirming the role of subjective choice is the most basic condition for achieving historical determinism. The relationship between the two is specifically expressed in the following:

First, many laws simultaneously govern and operate in human society. The effect of one law is always influenced by others, so that the effect of each law is interfered with to a certain extent. In this way, the specific manifestations of social laws produce diversity and uncertainty. For example, laws whereby productive forces determine production relations, the economic base determines superstructure, and social existence determines social consciousness do not mean that each production relationship is suitable for productive forces, each superstructure is suitable for the economic base, or each social consciousness is suitable for social existence. Rather, it means that production relations always change with productive forces; the superstructure with the economic base; and social consciousness with the social existence. The production relations suitable for the development of productive forces, the superstructure suitable for the development of the economic base, and social consciousness suitable for the development of social existence are not formed spontaneously, but are established through people's choice, leaving room for people to choose production relations, superstructure, and social consciousness. In the final analysis, the choice cannot violate the development requirements of productive forces, economic base, and social existence. Otherwise, the choice will eventually fail.

Second, in terms of the determinism of historical materialism, the intrinsic link in social processes revealed by social laws is not linear causality of the univocal determinism, but nonlinear causality of the probabilistic determinism. Therefore, social laws not only provide one possibility for people's activities, but a space of possibilities composed of multiple possibilities. Under established objective conditions, which possibility may be realized depends on voluntary activities of the subject, the choice by the subject, and the relationship among different subjects. For example, value determines price. However, the price is determined not only by value, but also by various other social factors such as supply and demand, so that commodities with the same value may be sold at different prices. The selection of same commodity with diverse prices depends on the choice of the subject. In this situation, people have the initiative and choice in formulating price policies and stipulating prices of commodities. Under certain historical conditions, different subjects often have different choices. Meanwhile, what or which subject's choices can be achieved depends on whether the choices between different subjects conform to the direction of historical development, and depends on the comparison of forces between different subjects.

Third, the realization of each possibility presents a variety of forms, namely a variety of specific modes and approaches. The selection of specific modes and approaches can show great initiative. These specific modes and approaches will differ, perhaps even diametrically, in the degree of realizing the subject's purpose and conforming to objective laws. However, only one possibility can be realized, that is, only one possibility can turn into reality. Whether the realization of this possibility is the best mode and approach for the subject's purpose depends on the correctness of the subject's cognition of objective laws and the extent to which the subject's initiative is developed. Choice plays a key role in realizing subjective initiative, which embodies people's independence, self-discipline, and freedom. The choices of subjects vary greatly, making history more colorful. The success or failure of the subjects' choices endows the historical process with twists and turns, so that the historical development of different countries and nationalities differs. Being able to make choices is a great human power, and is the source of endless creativity and the outstanding performance of humans as the dominator of all things. Our choice may be correct or wrong, and the right choice will bring joy and happiness, while the wrong choice will bring suffering and disaster. Therefore, we must cautiously make choices and assume responsibility for them. At no time should we forget our ability to choose, and lose ourselves in our victory over animals, nature, and other people. Our ability to choose is constrained by objective conditions at all times, by our practical abilities and levels of cognition, by irrational factors such as our will and emotions, and especially by our interests. These subjective and objective conditions are the preconditions that cannot be superseded by our choice.

Finally, the unity between subjective choice and objective laws comes from long and arduous exploration to improve human knowledge and practice. The longer and broader this exploration, the better the human knowledge and practice, consequently the better the aforesaid unity. The better this unity, the more likely the success of human practice. Engels pointed out:

> The further the particular sphere which we are investigating is removed from the economic sphere and approaches that of pure abstract ideology, the more shall we find it exhibiting accidents in its development, the more will its curve run in a zig-zag. So also you will find that the axis of this curve will approach more and more nearly parallel to the axis of the curve of economic development the longer the period considered and the wider the field dealt with.

The relationship between ideology and economic development is as such, and so is the relationship between subjective choice and objective laws. For example, to determine the goal of its economic reforms, China underwent a long exploration. Before China's reform and opening-up, a highly centralized economy was in place. This economy, albeit with its active role at the time, suffers numerous drawbacks. To replace this economy with a more effective one, China proposed to adopt the following: "planned economy as the mainstay and market economy as the supplement," "planned commodity economy based on public ownership," "the economy uniting plan and market," and "combining planned economy and market economy." In 1992, the 14th CPC National Congress declared that the objective of China's economic restructuring was a socialist market economy. This acknowledges the necessity that the market economy is non-leapable in social development. The perfection of China's new economic system will be a long and arduous process.

3.3.4 Freedom and necessity

The relation between freedom and necessity is closely linked with that between historical determinism and humans' capability to change the world. Freedom concerns subjective activities, which enable humans to change the world. Necessity concerns historical determinism, and governs the necessity, regularity, and causality in history. Unity between freedom and necessity implies unity between historical determinism and the human capability to change the world.

Inevitability and necessity mean the same and address laws and tendencies embedded in nature. In his *Speech in the Plenary Work Session of the Central Committee*, Mao Zedong said in 1962: "The so-called necessity gives the regularity of objective existence. Before we know it, our actions are unconscious and well-nigh blind."[22] Simply put, necessity is the objective law that governs the development of things, and historical necessity is the objective law that governs the development of social history.

Engels illuminated freedom and its relation with necessity in *Anti-Dühring*:

> Freedom does not consist in any dreamt-of independence from natural laws, but in the knowledge of these laws, and in the possibility this gives of systematically making them work towards definite ends. This holds good in relation both to the laws of external nature and to those which govern the bodily and mental existence of men themselves – two classes of laws which we can separate from each other at most only in thought but not in reality. Freedom of the will therefore means nothing but the capacity to make decisions with knowledge of the subject. Therefore the *freer* a man's judgment is in relation to a definite question, the greater is the *necessity* with which the content of this judgment will be determined; while the uncertainty, founded on ignorance, which seems to make an arbitrary choice among many different and conflicting possible decisions, shows precisely by this that it is not free, that it is controlled by the very object it should itself control. Freedom therefore consists in the control over ourselves and over external nature, a control founded on knowledge of natural necessity; it is therefore necessarily a product of historical development.[23]

Such is the relation between freedom and natural necessity, and between freedom and historical necessity. Borrowing Engels, Mao Zedong succinctly defined freedom: "Freedom understands necessity so as to transform the world."[24] Engels and Mao Zedong contend that freedom cannot be understood in itself, but through its relation with necessity. The former presupposes the latter. Freedom and its relation with necessity carry two implications. First, freedom is based on and finds its very existence in the understanding of necessity. Second, freedom is the practice of changing the objective world as based on the understanding of necessity. That is, the social actor, to be free, cannot rest on a mere understanding of objective necessity; s/he must use that understanding to guide his or her practical activities to change the objective world. Freedom encompasses both knowledge and practice. Therefore, freedom in social history entails recognition of the objective necessity of social history to guide the practice of changing social history.

3.4 Relation between interpreting and changing the world

A close connection exists between interpreting the world and changing it and between historical determinism and human capability to change the world. We may analyze this connection based on the 11th of Marx's *Theses on Feuerbach* written in 1845 spring. Marx said: "Philosophers have hitherto only interpreted the world in various ways; the point is to change it."[25] Some and perhaps many scholars in China and beyond thus interpret Marx's above words: the philosophy of all pre-Marxian philosophers had only "interpreted the world" while only Marxist philosophy claimed to "change the world." Some even dichotomize philosophy into that of "interpreting the world" and that of "changing the world." They believe that no philosophy other than Marxist philosophy represents the latter. This rather popular view, I argue, misinterprets and distorts Marx. The key here lies in understanding "philosophers" as meant by Marx. Does it refer to all or only specific philosophical schools before Marx? I argue for the latter, specifically the young Hegelians emerging during the disintegration of Hegelian philosophy. That is, these Hegelians only attempted to "interpret" the world with no effort of changing it. A discussion of this follows.

When criticizing French and British materialists and communists in *Holy Family*, Marx said:

> The criticism of the French and the English is not an abstract, preternatural personality beyond mankind; it is the real human activities of individuals who are active members of society and who suffer, feel, think and act as human beings. That is why their criticism is at the same time practical, their communism a socialism which gives practical, concrete measures and in which they do not just think but act even more, it is the living real criticism of existing society, the discovery of the causes of "the decay."[26]

In other words, the criticism by the French and British materialists and communists did not merely address ideas and thoughts or interpretations of the world. It advocated changing of existing society through revolutionary practices.

Engels concurred with Marx. In his manuscript *Dialectics of Nature*, Engels discussed the great thinkers, artists, scientists, philosophers, revolutionaries, and their activities to change the world since the Renaissance. Engels said,

> It was the greatest progressive revolution that mankind has so far experienced, a time which called for giants and produced giants—giants in power of thought, passion, and character, in universality and learning. The men who founded the modern rule of the bourgeoisie had anything but bourgeois limitations. On the contrary, the adventurous character of the time inspired them to a greater or less degree.

The heroes of that time had not yet come under the servitude of the division of labour, the restricting effects of which, with its production of one sidedness, we so often notice in their successors. But what is especially characteristic of them is that they almost all pursue their lives and activities in the midst of the contemporary movements, in the practical struggle; they take sides and join in the fight, one by speaking and writing, another with the sword, many with both. Hence the fullness and force of character that makes them complete men. Men of the study are the exception—either persons of second or third rank or cautious philistines who do not want to burn their fingers. At that time natural science also developed in the midst of the general revolution and was itself thoroughly revolutionary; it had to win in struggle its right of existence. Side by side with the great Italians from whom modern philosophy dates, it provided its martyrs for the stake and the prisons of the Inquisition.[27]

Engels' words indicate that the great figures since the Renaissance have engaged not only passively in the ideological critique of old systems, not only passively in the interpretation of the world, but also vigorously in the movement of their time. They used pens, swords, or both to criticize the actual revolutionary practices against the old society, and even dared their lives upon the guillotine and the gallows.

The French and British materialist philosophy not only interprets the world, but advocates changing it. Hegelian idealism, however, interprets, without attempting to change, the world. In *Ludwig Feuerbach and the End of Classical German Philosophy*, Engels criticized Hegelian philosophy, arguing that it starts with an absolute idea, walks through a series of links and another series of negation of negations, and yet finally returns to nothing but the same absolute idea.

> But at the end of the whole philosophy, a similar return to the beginning is possible only in one way. Namely, by conceiving of the end of history as follows: mankind arrives at the cognition of the self-same absolute idea, and declares that this cognition of the absolute idea is reached in Hegelian philosophy. And what applies to philosophical cognition applies also to historical practice. Mankind, which, in the person of Hegel, has reached the point of working out the absolute idea, must also in practice have gotten so far that it can carry out this absolute idea in reality. Hence the practical political demands of the absolute idea on contemporaries may not be stretched too far. And so we find at the conclusion of the Philosophy of Right that the absolute idea is to be realized in that monarchy based on social estates which Frederick William III so persistently but vainly promised to his subjects.[28]

When criticizing Hegelian thought and its "identity with being," Engels argued that Hegel's identification of thought with being is nothing but an absolute self-cognition, a thought of thought. Engels added that thought and being, for Hegel, are but different manifestations of the same absoluteness; the thing to be known is pre-embedded in the thought of it.

> But that in no way prevents Hegel from drawing the further conclusion from his proof of the identity of thing and being that his philosophy, because it is correct for his thinking, is therefore the only correct one, and that the identity

of thinking and being must prove its validity by mankind immediately translating his philosophy from theory into practice and transforming the whole world according to Hegelian principles. This is an illusion which he shares with well-nigh all philosophers.[29]

In other words, all philosophers, including pure idealists such as Hegel, dream of turning their philosophies into reality and changing the world according to their philosophies. The only differences lie in their methods of and the degree of success in changing the world.

For Feuerbach, it is not that he didn't address practice. He even criticized idealism on basis of practical ideas, to which he attached great value. He even incorporated practice into his epistemology. Beuerbach said: "The main shortcoming of idealism is that it only proposes and solves the problems of objectivity and subjectivity, the truth and non-authenticity of the world from a theoretical point of view."[30] Idealism does not understand that "practice will solve the problems that the theory cannot solve."[31] In his book *Materialism and Empirio-Criticism*, Lenin highly valued Feuerbach's practical viewpoint. Lenin said: "Feuerbach makes the sum-total of human practice the basis of the theory of knowledge."[32] However, Feuerbach regards practical activities as the dirty business of petty businesspeople for profit. To Feuerbach, theorization is the only real practical activity. He saw no significance in revolutionary practices. In *German Ideology*, Marx and Engels thus critiqued Feuerbach:

> In reality and for the practical materialist, i.e. the communist, it is a question of revolution is in the existing world, of practically attacking and changing existing things. When occasionally we find such views with Feuerbach, they are never more than isolated surmises and have much too little influence on his general outlook to be considered here as anything else than embryos capable of development.[33]

However, despite our arguments so far, we cannot claim that Feuerbach's philosophy merely interprets the world and negates the need to change the world.

Marx's words "Philosophers have hitherto only interpreted the world in various ways; the point is to change it," seen in Article 11 of *Theses on Feuerbach*, may be said about specific philosophers in a specific context from a specific perspective. First of all, the "philosophers" here do not refer to all philosophers before the birth of Marxist philosophy, but specifically to young Hegelians; second, the specific context here refers to the dark and tragic realities in Germany faced by young Hegelian philosophers at that time; and third, the specific perspective here is that young Hegelians only carried out philosophical and religious critiques, using their words against others', but dared not to confront Germany's dark reality with bold discussion of revolutionary practices. This is why Marx argued that young Hegelians only interpreted the world with no attempt to change it through revolutionary practices. It misunderstands Marx to claim that no philosophy other than Marxist philosophy advocates changing the world, and that philosophy is dichotomized into those that merely interpret the world and those that also attempt to change the world.

After our analyses so far, the following summary is offered concerning the relation between historical determinism and the human capability to change the world:

First, historical materialism is historical determinism, not historical nondeterminism. This is the first theoretical premise for examining the relation between historical determinism and human capability of changing the world. It is untenable to regard historical materialism as historical nondeterminism, which contradicts the essence of historical materialism.

Second, the determinism of historical materialism is a materialist dialectical determinism. It is essentially different from mechanical determinism, historical fatalism, or historical pre-determinism. This is the second theoretical premise in need of clarification to accurately assess the relation between historical determinism and the human possibility to change the world. Deniers and critics of the historical determinism of historical materialism mostly confuse it with mechanical determinism, historical fatalism, or historical pre-determinism. Typical examples include Karl Popper's *The Poverty of Historical Determinism*.

Third, historical determinism and human's possibility to change the world are two aspects of the same issue. These two are not only reconcilable but closely connected, internally united, and mutually premised. Any effort otherwise would be fundamentally wrong. Accepting the former while denying the latter leads to mechanical determinism or historical fatalism. Reversely, accepting the latter while denying the former leads to historical idealism or voluntarism.

Fourth, historical determinism believes that historical development has necessity, objective regularity, and causality. It is the prerequisite for humans to change the world and history through practical activities. If historical development has no necessity and objective regularity, if humans' practical activities are guided by no historical necessity and objective regularity, if humans are ignorant of the basic trend of historical development, then humans will not be able to determine the purpose and direction of their activities nor formulate plans for their future. Consequently, human activities become arbitrary, analogous to a messy horde of flies. Human activities as such won't effectively change the world or history. Catastrophes and misery may lie ahead to engender the demise of humankind itself.

Fifth, humans' subjective choice refers to their understanding of the necessity and objective regularity of historical development, which they use to guide their practical activities to change the world. It is the prerequisite for the operation of historical determinism. The necessity and objective regularity of historical development are neither a preconceived determination nor product of an unknown supra-human force. They give form to human activities and enable humans to change the world.

Notes

1 Han Zhen. (1992). *Introduction to the Western Philosophy of History*. Jinan, China: Shandong People's Press, 3.
2 Walsh, W. H. (1991). *Philosophy of History: An Introduction* (He Zhaowu & Zhang Wenjie, Trans.). Beijing, China: Social Sciences Academic Press.

3 *An Anthology of Marx and Engels* (Vol. 1). (2009). Beijing, China: People's Publishing House, 525.

4 *An Anthology of Marx and Engels* (Vol. 1). (2009). Beijing, China: People's Publishing House, 544.

5 *An Anthology of Marx and Engels* (Vol. 1). (2009). Beijing, China: People's Publishing House, 544–545.

6 *An Anthology of Marx and Engels* (Vol. 1). (2009). Beijing, China: People's Publishing House, 545.

7 *An Anthology of Marx and Engels* (Vol. 1). (2009). Beijing, China: People's Publishing House, 575–576.

8 *An Anthology of Marx and Engels* (Vol. 10). (2009). Beijing, China: People's Publishing House, 42–43.

9 *An Anthology of Marx and Engels* (Vol. 1). (2009). Beijing, China: People's Publishing House, 602.

10 *An Anthology of Marx and Engels* (Vol. 2). (2009). Beijing, China: People's Publishing House, 591–592.

11 *An Anthology of Marx and Engels* (Vol. 5). (2009). Beijing, China: People's Publishing House, 10.

12 *An Anthology of Marx and Engels* (Vol. 5). (2009). Beijing, China: People's Publishing House, 9–10.

13 *An Anthology of Marx and Engels* (Vol. 4). (2009). Beijing, China: People's Publishing House, 301.

14 *An Anthology of Marx and Engels* (Vol. 4). (2009). Beijing, China: People's Publishing House, 303. Emphasis added.

15 *An Anthology of Marx and Engels* (Vol. 4). (2009). Beijing, China: People's Publishing House, 304.

16 *An Anthology of Marx and Engels* (Vol. 4). (2009). Beijing, China: People's Publishing House, 302.

17 *An Anthology of Marx and Engels* (Vol. 2). (2009). Beijing, China: People's Publishing House, 470–471.

18 *Collected Works of Marx and Engels* (Vol. 4). (1958). Beijing, China: People's Publishing House, 149.

19 *An Anthology of Marx and Engels* (Vol. 9). (2009). Beijing, China: People's Publishing House, 300.

20 *Collected Works of Lenin—On Dialectical Materialism and Historical Materialism.* (2009). Beijing, China: People's Publishing House, 179.

21 *Selected Works of Mao Zedong.* (Vol. 2). (1991). Beijing, China: People's Publishing House, 478.

22 *Collected Works of Mao Zedong.* (Vol. 8) (1999). Beijing, China: People's Publishing House, 306.

23 *An Anthology of Marx and Engels* (Vol. 9). (2009). Beijing, China: People's Publishing House, 120. Emphasis added.

24 *Selected Works of Mao Zedong.* (Vol. 2). (1986). Beijing, China: People's Publishing House, 833.

25 *An Anthology of Marx and Engels* (Vol. 1). (2009). Beijing, China: People's Publishing House, 502.

26 *An Anthology of Marx and Engels* (Vol. 1). (2009). Beijing, China: People's Publishing House, 355.

27 *An Anthology of Marx and Engels* (Vol. 9). (2009). Beijing, China: People's Publishing House, 409, 409–410, 405.

28 *An Anthology of Marx and Engels* (Vol. 4). (2009). Beijing, China: People's Publishing House, 171.

29 *An Anthology of Marx and Engels* (Vol. 4). (2009). Beijing, China: People's Publishing House, 279.

30 Le Yanping. (1961). *The Interpretation of Ludwig Feuerbach and the End of Classical German Philosophy*. Shijiazhuang, China: Hebei People's Press, 256.
31 *Selected Readings of Feuerbac's Philosophical Works*. (1959). Beijing, China: SDX Joint Publishing Company, 248.
32 *Lenin's Monographs on Materialism and Empirio-Criticism*. (2009). Beijing, China: People's Publishing House, 49.
33 *An Anthology of Marx and Engels* (Vol. 1). (2009). Beijing, China: People's Publishing House, 527.

4 Historical progress and its measure

With rapid developments in modern society, people have felt the general and tremendous impact of social transformation. "Social progress" has become a hot topic in scholarly discussions. But what is social progress? How to properly measure it? How to correctly assess the (choice of) costs in the pursuit of social progress? These are debatable questions awaiting answers. To effectively answer these questions, we need to define "historical progress" and investigate the evolution of relevant theories of Marx and Engels. Such investigation will deepen our appreciation of Marx and Engels' theory on social progress in Eastern and ancient societies.

4.1 The conception of historical progress

A review of history indicates that historical progress is a concept recent in history. Despite its origin in ancient society, the concept of social progress was never dominant in ancient ideology, either in the East or in the West. However, history is often remembered as the "good old days" that frequently eclipse the contemporary experience. The concept of historical progress is a product of modern thoughts. Francis Bacon (British) and René Descartes (French) made a preliminary demonstration of historical progress from the perspective of improving human's cognition and faculty to control their practice. After that, it was the French Enlightenment that contributed most to the conception of historical progress. Representative scholars such as Anne Robert Jacques Turgot, Marquis de Condorcet, Denis Diderot, Voltaire, Montesquieu, Quesnay, Holbach, and Jean le Rond d'Alembert all held the belief that human beings can gradually learn how to control nature and subject it to their service. This could be done with enhanced rationality and knowledge, which enhance material life, legislature and political reforms, and aesthetics and morality. In short, the French Enlightenment advocates rationality, believes in education and enlightenment, and regards them as a guarantee for continued progress of humanity. This is the Enlightenment's fundamental view on historical progress. Marx and Engels critically inherited French Enlightenment ideas concerning historical progress, and conceived their own view of "historical progress based on historical materialism." Marx said: "The concept of progress [is] not to be conceived in the usual abstractness."[1] Guided by

Marx and Engels' thoughts on historical progress and through the lens of human history, we can conceptualize historical progress as follows.

4.1.1 Historical progress is an upward and forward movement

History is not a repetitive or stagnant process, but an upward and forward tendency of sustained advancement. The decisive power behind historical progress is humans' practical activities. To meet their basic survival needs, humans have engaged in material production throughout time. On the one hand, they have created a strong material foundation (e.g., productive forces and social systems) for human progress. On the other hand, for the same purpose humans have nurtured their talents and potentiality in cognition, aesthetics, and moral practice. In other words, confronting a powerful nature, humans have built a humanized world, one of their own, tremendously enriched with material wealth and spiritual creations. Humans' ceaseless experiences and intentions propel their pursuit of happiness and perfection.

Historical progress can be measured quantitatively by the size of the economy and material wealth, and qualitatively by human civilization, capability, and individuality. Generally, compared with the mindless state of scavenging for crude food in ancient times, human history has undoubtedly and significantly ascended to the better.

4.1.2 Historical progress is tortuous and iterative

One understanding of historical progress is extreme optimism. In this view, history moves forward as if along a straight error-free line, at a sustained pace, fulfilling all of its preset goals. Such an idealistic pattern unfortunately is nonexistent. According to Marx, "In spite of the pretensions of 'Progress', continual retrogressions and circular movements occur."[2] Human civilization largely started with the recognition and fulfillment of individual desires. The clan chiefs or tribal chiefs exploited their given power to expropriate public properties of the primitive communes and tribes, giving rise to private ownership and classes and countries. Every major step however long in the evolution of human civilization is more or less a process of gestation, iteration, turmoil, and pain. No historical progress is free of repetitive twists and turns. Such twists and turns may include earthquakes, hurricanes, desertification, and tornadoes, often leading to hiatuses in and the demise of certain human civilizations. Modern human history has been full of chaos: The "sheep-eating-people" Enclosure Movement in early capitalistic England; the two brutal world wars in which countries fought for monopolization over colonies and global markets; the subversive activities by some superpower carried out in small and vulnerable nations and countries, in the name of fighting terrorism; and damages humans have wrecked on the environment in order to extract resources. All of these have led to resource shortages, energy crises, environmental pollution, greenhouse effects, reduction of biodiversity, and destruction of the planet's ecology. Humans might have destroyed what took nature a billion years to produce.

Historical progress has cost humankind a high price. Therefore, historical progress should not be understood simplistically, mechanically, or linearly. History does not follow such a formula whereby humanity, once boarding the train of communism, is well on its way to fulfilling its dreams. History inevitably is an arduous process of frustrations, failures, and relapses into the old system before appearance of the new.

Historical progress has always been achieved with sacrifices and struggles, which, however, have taught humanity indelible lessons to compel further progress.

4.1.3 *Historical progress embodies both facts and values*

It is not difficult to recognize the objective necessity of historical progress. The question is: How do we decipher this objective necessity? According to one view, history has its intrinsic logic, force, trajectory, and mechanism, all independent of human subjectivity. This view separates historical objectivity from human subjectivity, necessity from fortuity. Historical progress in its actuality is neither the result of an external purpose (as argued by Vico, Kant, and Hegel) nor is it intrinsically automatic, but is compelled by the human subject's practice and activities. Historical progress is ultimately human progress, the constant externalization of the internal human force. The human need for survival propels material production. In this process, humans have to constantly adjust their relation with nature and with each other in order to enhance their productivity to meet their increasing needs. In the evolution of human relationship, those in servitude aspire to be free and to expand their freedom. In the process of interacting with each other and with nature, humans constantly enlarge their self-understanding, their emotion and rationality, their cognition and practice. It is the dialectical process between limitation and potentiality that fuels historical progress.

As an objective process, historical progress has never been separate from humans' subjective creation. The labor and creation of human beings—the subject of history—play a fundamental and decisive role in history. In addition, it is particularly important to emphasize the value assessment of historical progress. That is to say, the assessment of historical progress is a human act, an act by the subject of history. Without human goals and value assessment, historical progress is a hollow concept. History does not interpret itself, but is interpreted by the human subject according to the latter's standards and values. Therefore, historical progress embodies both facts and values.

4.1.4 *Historical progress is the dialectical unity of accumulation and transformation*

Any historical progress requires certain material prerequisites and a certain level of productive forces. The establishment of all production relations and social systems requires a quantifiable material base, without which no corresponding historical progress can be achieved. However, historical progress is not purely of material wealth, but comprehends economics, politics, and culture. In its highest form, it is the full and free development of the individual.

The process of social evolution and historical progress represents dialectical unity between quantity and quality. At a particular level of quantitative accumulation (e.g., per capita GDP of US$3,000 in China), social development may enter a critical juncture. As a result, significant social contradictions or challenges as well as development opportunities will emerge. If China can successfully resolve its historical challenges, it may achieve its goal of becoming a moderately prosperous society. According to the Inverted-U Hypothesis of American economist and statistician Simon Smith Kuznets, a country, in order to realize its own economic development, must carry out the development strategy of uneven distribution in a certain period, inevitably leading to increasing inequality between the rich and the poor. Fortunately, with the further development of productive forces and further increase of social wealth, income distribution will re-balance, so that the sharp social conflicts will be resolved eventually. The eventual resolution of social inequality may represent another form of social progress. In short, historical progress is a continual and interruptive process uniting quantitative accumulation and qualitative transformation.

4.1.5 Historical progress is a long process

As mentioned above, historical progress embodies both facts and values, both quantitative accumulation and qualitative transformation. Historical progress is a long process based on the creative activities of human production and labor practice, the development of productive forces, the transformation of production relations, the development of social culture, and the improvement of human qualities and capabilities. As such, the idealism of dramatic advance should be abandoned. Historical progress is inevitably a dialectical and not so rosy process. It involves conflict, frustration, repetition, and even retrogression. Therefore, historical progress must be understood as a protracted winding course. Many thinkers have attempted to render unambiguous explanations of the historical process once and for all, including the development of science and technology, the infinite perfection of human nature, or the full realization of freedom and equality. Many politicians and strategists have adopted complete equality and harmony between people, an infinite and sublime human spiritual world, as the ideal guiding principle of governance. Such idealism has failed due to major defects in practice. It regards historical progress as a perpetual continuation rather than interruptive accumulation. The ideal of historical progress can never be realized free of the limitations of human values and social conditions. The dialectic between ideal and reality dictates that the ideal must be materialized in the medium of reality, that the ideal, once materialized, no longer represents the ideal and thus awaits further development in a different medium of social reality.

Therefore, historical progress is an upward objective process based on humans' subjective activities, a process of conflicts and costs, of qualitative accumulation and qualitative transformation, and of the dialectical progression between the real and the ideal. In short, historical progress unites the subjective and the objective, the quantitative and the qualitative, human value and physical reality. Dialectically, it propels humanity toward greater liberty and maturity.

4.2 The price of historical progress

All historical progress is closely tied with and achieved at a price. The former compensates for the latter. No historical progress is free of a price.

4.2.1 Essence of the price of historical progress

The price of historical progress denotes human work and sacrifices and negative consequences incurred for such progress. Unlike the energy loss in the motion of matter, the price of historical progress exists only amid historical activities and is manifested in the form of losses and negative consequences, which, however, are incurred for the express purpose of historical progress. The cost incurred other than for the purpose of progress is not included in our definition. Specifically, the cost of historical progress includes expenses, value depreciation, human sacrifices, historical errors, and negative consequences therein.

Cost refers to the input and efforts in human historical activities. Historical progress involves costs for both the subject and the object. As subjects of history, humans are the initiator and regulator of historical activities. They have to expend physical strength and brain power, consume lives, and often inhibit and restrain personal needs in order to succeed in their cause. As for the historical object, the cost includes the consumption of raw materials and natural resources, the expense of labor means, and the disintegration of active objects and so on. Cost is the price that humans have to pay for all historical progress. This price is inevitable, but humans may strive to decrease costs, reduce input, and increase output, in order to obtain greater historical progress at a lower cost.

In historical activities, humans are both the end and the means. As a means, humans must undergo value depreciation and sacrifice in historical activities. For example, human beings start from barbarism, and in the effort of overcoming barbarism, enter into civilization and progress. In this process, they had to use crude and savage methods: "it achieved them by setting in motion the lowest instincts and passions in man and developing them at the expense of all his other abilities."

> Since civilization is founded on the exploitation of one class by another class, its whole development proceeds in a constant contradiction. Every step forward in production is at the same time a step backwards in the position of the oppressed class, that is, of the great majority. Whatever benefits some necessarily injures the others; every fresh emancipation of one class is necessarily a new oppression for another class.[3]

Historically and even now, incompatibility exists within the development of different aspects of humanity and between the development of the individual and the development of humanity as a whole. The development of one aspect inevitably hurts another. The development of the individual inevitably hurts the collective. Only in the future communist society will the development of each individual become a condition for the development of all. Mistakes in history result from subjective human reasons. As the historical subject, the human finds it impossible to be completely correct in all cognitive and practical activities. Historical mistakes are the inevitable price and lay the necessary foundation for historical progress. Reflection upon mistakes enhances humans' self-awareness and their capability to better foresee and handle the future.

All historical activities are dialectical processes encompassing both pros and cons. Even well-considered plans have negative consequences, differing only in degree and duration and perhaps manifested at different times. As common in history, good wishes do not always end in good results, because limitations are many and human needs diverse. Human learning in the process may increase but will never eradicate negative consequences from historical activities. This may remain the case even in the future communist society.

4.2.2 The necessity of the costs of historical progress

The costs for historical development are inevitable due to human, natural, and social limitations. The transformation and enhancement of nature and society and production are foundational for and symbolic of human progress. Human beings have invested energy and wisdom, blood and sweat. On the other hand, the process has also resulted in environmental pollution, energy depletion, resource scarcity, and retaliations from nature. In the field of social relations, from the primitive society to the capitalist society, human development is realized at the sacrifice of individuals. The class society subjects one class to another's servitude, oppressing and alienating the former. Human progress embeds a cost along its every step.

Social costs in historical progress are necessarily omnipresent. Such costs may be coerced by one group upon another, by irrationality inherent in a social relation, or by the fact that the subject is not yet made master of his or her own service. Absence of choice has a price. There is always a gap between human needs and the degree of satisfaction of those needs. In a society of low productivity, the satisfaction of basic human needs has required the sacrifice of many non-basic human needs. Social and individual development is always a graduated and prioritized process in which the development of one thing may lead to the suppression of another.

The costs for historical progress assume different forms and characteristics at different times. In the primitive society, such costs derive mainly from the severe harshness of nature working against human frailty. In a class society, one class develops at the expense of another. In capitalism, one country or region develops at the expense of another. Only in communism will humanity as a whole attain its free and full development.

4.2.3 A scientific conception of price

The inevitable cost of historical progress is paid in a manner and amount determined by human activities. Here, we must guard against two tendencies: Romanticism and pessimism. Romanticists notice development but ignore the price or treat the price as a natural thing. Pessimists are frustrated with the costs of progress, especially dramatic costs during social transformation. The so-called price awareness refers to the attitudes and intention of the historical subject toward gains and losses, advantages and disadvantages in historical development. It is an important part of the subject's ideology. The subjective attitudes toward costs of historical progress differ dramatically among different individuals. This attitude significantly affects human activities and the (scope of) human role in historical development. Proper human activities come from proper conception of historical costs.

Price awareness encompasses costs, pros and cons, risks, and sacrifices. It assesses the manpower, material resources, and financial resources needed for human activities. The historical subject must note that all production entails investment or cost. Proper investment is prerequisite for achieving desired results. Price awareness evaluates the necessity and propriety of costs.

Awareness of the pros and cons positively acknowledges the dialectical duality of pros and cons. This awareness facilitates the choice between a correct attitude toward, and predictions about pros and cons. It holistically assesses all factors and links within human activities and acts accordingly. It also *proactively* evaluates short- and long-term consequences and the dynamic interplay between cause and consequence to guide predictions about future.

Risk awareness is the entrepreneurial initiative in the presence of risks and is neither conservativism nor defeatism. It actively heeds and defuses risks and thus differs from a gambler's adventurism.

The spirit of sacrifice transcends one's finite self to embrace the infinite cause of human justice and progress. It is neither an idler nor a suicidal daredevil. It cherishes life but fears no death; it is ready for sacrifice but wary of unnecessary sacrifice. It strives for the best at the lowest price.

4.2.4 Correctly choosing the price

Marxism dialectically views the relationship between the objective inevitability and subjective selectivity of historical progress. On the one hand, it affirms that the price of historical progress is objectively inevitable; on the other hand, it acknowledges that humans' choice of price plays an important role. When choosing the price, the subject assesses current historical conditions and all possible configurations of costs and success. The selectivity of historical progress is largely the selectivity of price.

In the socialist modernization, we should dialectically view the price. On the one hand, we must give top priority to development. Development is an absolute necessity. We should recognize the necessity and rationality of the price of development. On the other hand, we must uphold the principle of rationality and moderation and be vigilant against and prevent excessive price. We should reduce and control social pressure and contradictions caused by unnecessary price, defuse all social issues during social development, and maintain social stability. Humans' choice of price can reduce the price and optimize development. The basic principle of price choice is "the greater of two benefits and the lesser of two costs." That is, the subject's conscious choice can lessen and shorten the pain of history, reduce unnecessary endeavors and losses, and save the cost of social development, thus optimizing historical progress. This is prominently seen in transformative developments in history based on conscious price selectivity. Price selectivity enhances the subject's sense of historical initiative and social responsibility over inevitable costs.

Progress is the main theme and general trend in the long river of history. Although there have been endeavors, sacrifices, twists and turns, and even retrogressions in historical movements, progress remains as the dominant and basic trend. The price is always subsidiary to and supportive of historical progress. With the development of productive forces and various social relations, people will pay an increasingly smaller price for increasingly greater progress. In the communist society, humanity will fully eliminate irrational and unnecessary prices. Marx thus spoke of the material production in the communist society:

> [The] socialised man, the associated producers, rationally regulating their interchange with Nature, bringing it under their common control, instead of being ruled by it as by the blind forces of Nature; and achieving this with the least expenditure of energy and under conditions most favourable to, and worthy of, their human nature.[4]

4.3 Two measures of historical evaluation and their relation

Marx and Engels measured historical progress in two ways: The historical measure and the value measure. The former is also called the objective scale, external scale, and scientific scale; the latter the subjective scale, intrinsic scale, and moral scale.

The historical measure evaluates a social system or phenomenon by reviewing whether it accords with the inevitability and objective regularity of historical development, whether it meets the collective interests of humanity, and whether it coincides with their aspiration and requirements. The historical measure has two basic requirements. First, we should examine a social system or phenomenon based on the entire process of its occurrence and development rather than based on a static and unchanging condition. Second, we should evaluate a social system or social phenomenon from the conditions of the historical era to which it belongs rather than from present conditions and standards. To evaluate historical progress by the historical measure, we should view things from the perspective of history, place all social systems and social phenomena within its historical context, and dialectically analyze, research, and evaluate them based on their historical conditions.

The value measure refers to the scale and basis for judging the value, nature, and size of a social system or a social phenomenon. It is determined by the pursuit of interest, the structure of demands, the level of development, and the social relations of the evaluator. The value measure varies with (the practical activities and social lives of) historical evaluators and has distinct subjectivity.

The historical measure and the value measure are obviously different. The former is unidimensional while the latter is multidimensional. The historical measure unidimensionally evaluates a social system or phenomenon by reviewing whether it meets the interests of humanity as a whole, whether it coincides with the aspirations and requirements of all humankind, and whether it promotes the development of the collective. If so, the social system and phenomenon is progressive; otherwise, retrogressive or reactionary. In short, the historical measure considers the interests, aspirations, and demands of all humanity rather than those of specific individuals, classes, strata, and social groups. In human history, a new social system may benefit even the class, stratum, and individual that comes out the worst. Engels explained this phenomenon in *Anti-Dühring* by the example of the slave society that replaced the primitive society. He said:

> In the historical conditions of the ancient world, and particularly of Greece, the advance to a society based on class antagonisms could be accomplished only in the form of slavery. This was an advance even for the slaves; the prisoners of war, from whom the mass of the slaves was recruited, now at least saved their lives, instead of being killed as they had been before, or even roasted, as at a still earlier period.[5]

The multidimensionality of the value measure means that different individuals and social classes may assess the same social system or phenomenon differently or even oppositely. Some may consider it progressive or innovative, while others, backward or conservative. For example, in class society, evaluations of slavery by the slave-owner and the slave may be diametrical; the feudal lord class and the peasant class have contrary opinions about the feudal system; and in the capitalist society, the bourgeoisie and the proletariat think totally differently about the capitalist system.

The relationship between the two measures of historical progress is rather intricate. Historical materialism elaborates this relationship mainly from two perspectives.

First, regarding the general trend of historical development, the two measures are consistent. With the development of productive forces, people's interests, aspirations, and demands are increasingly being met. In the class society, when a new system of exploitation has emerged, the interests, aspirations and demands of the exploiting class are better satisfied than before, and so are those of the exploited class to a lesser degree. With the continuous enhancement of the productive forces and changes in the production relations, the living conditions of all people have been improved, human development has been advanced, the personal bondage relations have been weakened, and human freedom has been promoted. In the class society, conditions of both the exploiting and the exploited classes have been improved, though to different degrees. In his *Anti-Dühring*, Engels said:

> So long as a mode of production still describes an ascending curve of development, it is enthusiastically welcomed even by those who come off worst from its corresponding mode of distribution. This was the case with the English workers in the beginnings of modern industry. And even while this mode of production remains normal for society, there is, in general, contentment with the distribution, and if objections to it begin to be raised, these come from within the ruling class itself (Saint-Simon, Fourier, Owen) and find no response whatever among the exploited masses.[6]

Therefore, the evaluations made respectively by the historical measure and value measure will eventually reach the same goal and achieve unification in the holistic development of social life. For this unification, two thoughts of Marx and Engels should be brought to attention:

To begin with, the development of productive forces equates to that of humanity. Economists used to interpret productive forces as an increase in economic development, a means to meet human needs for survival and development, or a certain level of technology and production tools, without highlighting the dominant position of humanity in productive forces. For example, classical economists attached great importance to the issue of productive forces, but they elaborated it mainly from the perspective of production efficiency and increase of national wealth. Unlike classical economists, Friedrich List (a German economist contemporary with Marx) acknowledged the human role in developing productive forces. However, he merely regarded humans as the labor force and a living factor of production and did not truly establish the dominant and true position of the human in social historical activities. The revolutionary changes made by Marx on the issue have for the first time linked productive forces with the essential power of humanity. Marx believed that the development of productive forces is due to the development of humans' essential power. Therefore, the development of the productive force is not merely an enlargement of material things outside of the human, but a result of enlarged human potential and value. Here the historical measure and the value measure are completely unified, not irrelevant or antithetical to each other.

In addition, we should evaluate the progressiveness of a social system or phenomenon not abstractly but within the concrete historical context. For instance, slavery would be condemned by a modern society. However, historically, it represented advancement over its predecessor. Engels in *Anti-Dühring* said:

Without slavery, no Greek state, no Greek art and science; without slavery, no Roman Empire. But without the basis laid by Hellenism and the Roman Empire, also no modern Europe. We should never forget that our whole economic, political and intellectual development presupposes a state of things in which slavery was as necessary as it was universally recognized. In this sense we are entitled to say: Without the slavery of antiquity no modern socialism.[7]

This confirms the progressiveness of the slavery society which represented an ascending curve of history. From the perspective of the historical measure, slavery has its inevitability and rationality in the course of history. Engels also affirmed the progressiveness of the slavery society in terms of the value measure, which we have already discussed above. It follows that these two measures of historical progress do not contradict each other considering humanity as a whole. When we talk about historical progress, we must have an appropriate frame of reference. An abstract and general discussion of social progress may not shed much light.

Second, regarding a specific stage or period of historical development, there are inconsistencies between the two measures. When observing and evaluating a particular historical phenomenon of a particular period, the conclusions drawn by the value measure and by the historical measure may contradict each other. Such inconsistency comes from the intrinsic contradiction in a society—better but still inadequate productive forces. At a certain stage of the productive forces, human progress is often manifested as the development of some people at the expense of others. How? The development of the productive forces will inevitably lead to the spontaneous division of labor and fixed specializations. On the one hand, division of labor promotes productivity and progress. On the other hand, it gradually fragments social structures and makes social functions increasingly specialized, leading to three major differences and class antagonism. The spontaneous division of labor has markedly enhanced the overall capabilities of human beings but also made individual activities and capabilities stagnant, lopsided, and deformed. Each and every qualitative change in the spontaneous division of labor and the productive forces will necessarily result in major changes in the ownership system, bringing about the decline of the old historical subject and the rise of a new one. When the spontaneous division of labor is replaced by the conscious division of labor (or "smart division of labor") as will be seen in the communist society, individuals with free and comprehensive development will emerge, and the coordination and unity between the two measures of social progress will be achieved.

4.4 The shift of Marx's focus in the historical measure

Marx's thoughts on the two measures of historical progress and their interrelationship differed in different historical periods. He sometimes used both and other times only one of them. His focus on the historical measure varied based on the actual needs of historical evaluation. We will discuss his shift of focus in three historical periods.

4.4.1 In the early 1850s

In the early 1850s, Marx evaluated historical progress by combining the two measures. In his 1853 articles (*The British Rule in India* and *The Future Results of British Rule in India*), Marx severely criticized the heinous crimes committed by Western colonialists in the East. He argued that the catastrophe brought by the British to Hindustan was far more severe than what the Hindustanis had suffered in the past. He also elaborated on the primitiveness, brutality, and backwardness of the Eastern society and believed that the destruction of the Eastern social structures caused by Western colonialists was a real social revolution in the East, which promoted the progress of the Eastern society.

At that time, Marx believed that the profound hypocrisy and inherent barbarism of bourgeois civilization were laid bare once we shifted our attention from its home where it assumed respectable forms, to the colonies where it went naked. The colonists cruelly slaughtered the Eastern peoples, took the slaughter as a pleasure, and perpetrated their barbarous nature upon the Eastern peoples. The colonists' hands were covered with the blood of the Eastern peoples. Marx added,

> Sickening as it must be to human feeling to witness those myriads of industrious patriarchal and inoffensive social organizations disorganized and dissolved into their units, thrown into a sea of woes, and their individual members losing at the same time their ancient form of civilization, and their hereditary means of subsistence, we must not forget that these idyllic village-communities, inoffensive though they may appear, had always been the solid foundation of Oriental despotism, that they restrained the human mind within the smallest possible compass, making it the unresisting tool of superstition, enslaving it beneath traditional rules, depriving it of all grandeur and historical energies. We must not forget the barbarian egotism which, concentrating on some miserable patch of land, had quietly witnessed the ruin of empires, the perpetration of unspeakable cruelties, the massacre of the population of large towns, with no other consideration bestowed upon them than on natural events, itself the helpless prey of any aggressor who deigned to notice it at all. We must not forget that this undignified, stagnatory [sic], and vegetative life, that this passive sort of existence evoked on the other part, in contradistinction, wild, aimless, unbounded forces of destruction and rendered murder itself a religious rite in Hindustan. We must not forget that these little communities were contaminated by distinctions of caste and by slavery, that they subjugated man to external circumstances instead of elevating man the sovereign of circumstances, that they transformed a self-developing social state into never changing natural destiny, and thus brought about a brutalizing worship of nature.

Here, Marx's analysis of the Eastern society and its development trajectory is particularly noteworthy: First, Marx comprehensively investigated the relationship between colonialists and Eastern society through the historical measure and the value measure. Investigated from the value measure, the Western colonialists carried out a brutal plunder and slaughter on Eastern peoples, which Marx severely condemned. From the historical measure, he affirmed that Western colonialists' destruction of the traditional and backward social structure of the East played a positive role in the development of Eastern society. Second, Marx did not investigate social conflicts between the East and the West from the perspective of national sovereignty and national interests. Instead, he focused on deep issues related to the development of Eastern society from the perspective of world history and the destiny of the entire humankind, such as, what is the essence of the backwardness of Eastern society? What are root causes of the backwardness of Eastern society? Why have these ancient civilizations, with their long history and great geophysical resources, lagged behind the West in modern times? How can these Eastern countries break out of traditional constraints and embark on a new path? Marx posited that the root cause of the backwardness of the Eastern society lies in its own social structure. The trinity of the rural commune, state-owned land, and authoritarianism locked the Asian society in an extraordinary stability. Despite political changes taking place there and the constant change of government, the social structure remained unchanged. After studying the process of Western capitalism's invasion of Asia, Marx foresaw the new birth of Asia. He found that the ultra-stable triadic social structure of Asia might fall apart under the impact of the capitalist mode of production. The barbarism, primitiveness, and backwardness of the ancient civilization that had lasted for thousands of years may be transformed by the industrial civilization of Western capitalism. Therefore, the British invasion of India served as a bridge and link, and the European rule of Asia also provided an opportunity for the new birth of Asian society. Marx said:

> England, it is true, in causing a social revolution in Hindostan, was actuated only by the vilest interests, and was stupid in her manner of enforcing them. But that is not the question. The question is, can mankind fulfil its destiny without a fundamental revolution in the social state of Asia? If not, whatever may have been the crimes of England she was the unconscious tool of history in bringing about that revolution.

England thus "produced the greatest, and to speak the truth, the only social revolution ever heard of in Asia," "England has to fulfil a double mission in India: one destructive, the other regenerating – the annihilation of old Asiatic society and the laying of the material foundations of Western society in Asia."[8]

Marx also pointed out that the role of the revolutionary changes carried out by Western colonialists in India was very limited. It would neither liberate the people nor fundamentally improve their living conditions. Marx said:

> The Indians will not reap the fruits of the new elements of society scattered among them by the British bourgeoisie, till in Great Britain itself the now ruling classes shall have been supplanted by the industrial proletariat, or till the Hindus themselves shall have grown strong enough to throw off the English yoke altogether.

This is because the liberation of the people and the improvement of living conditions depend not only on the development of productive forces, but also on whether the people owned the productive forces. The colonialists can only create material preconditions for the liberation of the Eastern people and the improvement of their living conditions, but they do translate into immediate reality.

> When a great social revolution shall have mastered the results of the bourgeois epoch, the market of the world and the modern powers of production, and subjected them to the common control of the most advanced people, then only will human progress cease to resemble that hideous, pagan idol, who would not drink the nectar but from the skulls of the slain.[9]

Simply put, it is only by overthrowing capitalism and colonialism as well as realizing socialism and communism throughout the world that the liberation of people and improvement of living conditions can be realized.

4.4.2 From the mid-1850s to mid-1870s

From the mid-1850s to mid-1870s, the middle-aged Marx evaluated historical progress by combining the historical measure and the value measure. Here are some examples.

First, Marx discussed the serious discrepancy between the historical measure and the value measure in the capitalist era. His *Speech at the Anniversary of the People's Paper*, published on April 14, 1856, is typical of this view. He believed that on the one hand, from the historical measure, capitalism promoted productivity and science and technology, and created enormous material wealth and social development; on the other hand, from the value measure, the capitalistic use of productivity and science and technology had brought disasters to the working class and the laboring people, causing human alienation, value depreciation and moral decline, and hindering the liberation and development of people. He said:

In our days, everything seems pregnant with its contrary: Machinery, gifted with the wonderful power of shortening and fructifying human labour, we behold starving and overworking it; The newfangled sources of wealth, by some strange weird spell, are turned into sources of want; The victories of art seem bought by the loss of character. At the same pace that mankind masters nature, man seems to become enslaved to other men or to his own infamy. Even the pure light of science seems unable to shine but on the dark background of ignorance. All our invention and progress seem to result in endowing material forces with intellectual life, and in stultifying human life into a material force. This antagonism between modern industry and science on the one hand, modern misery and dissolution on the other hand; this antagonism between the productive powers and the social relations of our epoch is a fact, palpable, overwhelming, and not to be controverted.[10]

This discrepancy between the historical measure and the value measure can only be eliminated by the proletarian revolution to overthrow the bourgeois rule and replace it with a socialist society.

Second, Marx explained the combination and unity of the historical measure and the value measure from the relationship between the development of all mankind and that of individuals. In *Theories of Surplus Value*, Marx spoke highly of Ricardo's idea of taking productivity as the principal measure of economic phenomena. Marx said,

> Ricardo, rightly for his time, regards the capitalist mode of production as the most advantageous for production in general, as the most advantageous for the creation of wealth. He wants *production for the sake of production* and this with *good reason* (emphasis added).

Because "production for its own sake means nothing but the development of human productive forces, in other words the *development of the richness of human nature as an end in itself* (emphasis added)." Marx believed that, scientifically speaking, Ricardo's idea was both honest and necessary. It is unimportant to Ricardo whether the advance of the productivity destroys land ownership or the workers or devalues the capital of the industrial bourgeoisie. Ricardo's conception is, on the whole, in the interests of the *industrial bourgeoisie*; things are good so far as they coincide with productivity and efficiency of human labor. Sismondi blamed Ricardo sadly and believed that "the development of the species must be *arrested* (emphasis added) in order to safeguard the welfare of the individual, so that, for instance, no war may be waged in which at all events some individuals perish." Marx held that Sismondi did not understand that at a certain stage, the development of the entirety of humanity takes place at the cost of some individuals, or even of the entire class and nation. Only part of humanity, especially the excellent part, develops first. This is the only way for the eventual development of the entirety of humanity. Marx pointed out:

> They reveal a failure to understand the fact that, although at first the development of the capacities of the human species takes place at the cost of the majority of human individuals and even classes, in the end it breaks through this contradiction and coincides with the development of the individual; the higher development of individuality is thus only achieved by a historical process during which individuals are sacrificed for the interests of the species in the human kingdom, as in the animal and plant kingdoms, always assert themselves at the cost of the interests of individuals, because these interests of the species coincide only with the *interests of certain individuals*, and it is this coincidence which constitutes the strength of these privileged individuals.[11]

Third, through an analysis of the role of crimes and criminals, Marx explained the significance of unifying the historical measure with the value measure. In *The Fable of the Bees: or, Private Vices, Public Benefits*, the British satirical and democratic ethics writer, doctor, and economist Bernard Mandeville stated:

> That what we call Evil in this World, Moral as well as Natural, is the grand Principle that makes us Sociable Creatures, the solid Basis, *the Life and Support of all Trades and Employments* (emphasis added) without exception;

there we must look for the true origin of all Arts and Sciences; and the moment Evil ceases, the Society must he spoiled if not totally dissolved.

In *Economic Manuscripts of 1861–1863*, Marx cited Mandeville and gave him high marks. Marx held that "Mandeville had already shown that every possible kind of occupation is productive." "Only Mandeville was of course infinitely bolder and more honest than the philistine apologists of bourgeois society."[12] Marx developed Mandeville's thought from the perspective of social division of labor and social production. Marx believed that crime is a kind of evil. It is a social phenomenon that exists at a certain stage of historical development. There is no doubt that it is not conducive to social development. People should neither praise nor condone crimes. They cannot say that crimes will not disappear even if social development is at an advanced level, nor that once crimes disappear in the future, society will be destroyed. At the same time, we must also see that at a certain stage of social development, such as in capitalist society, the existence of criminals can lead to the emergence of new types of jobs and industries in social production, and provide additional employment opportunities, all of which become new subjects to observe and research. Marx said, as "a philosopher produces ideas, a poet poem, a clergyman sermons, a professor compendia," "a criminal produces crimes." If we look a little closer at the connection between this latter branch of production and society as a whole, "we shall rid ourselves of many prejudices."[13]

(1) The criminal produces not only crimes but also criminal law, and with this also the professor who gives lectures on criminal law and the inevitable syllabi in which this same professor throws his lectures onto the general market as "commodities." This brings not only economic benefits to these professors, but also happiness to people.

(2) The criminal produces the whole of the police and of criminal justice, constables, judges, executioners, juries, etc. All these different lines of business, which form equally many categories of labor, develop different capacities of the human spirit, and create new needs and new ways of satisfying them. For example, "torture alone has given rise to the most ingenious mechanical inventions, and employed many honourable craftsmen in the production of its instruments."[14]

(3) The criminal produces an impression, partly moral and partly tragic, as the case may be, and in this way renders a "service" by arousing the moral and aesthetic feelings of the public. As objects of literature and art, criminal behavior also produces art, belles-lettres, such as novels, and even tragedies, as not only Müllner's *Schuld* and Schiller's *Räuber*, but also *Oedipus* and *Richard the Third*.[15]

(4) In a capitalistic society, the criminal breaks the monotony and everyday security of bourgeois life. In this way he keeps it from stagnation, and gives rise to that uneasy tension and instability without which even the spur of competition would get blunted. Thus he stimulates the productive forces. While crime takes a part of the surplus population off the labor market and thus

reduces competition among the laborers—up to a certain point preventing wages from falling below the minimum—the struggle against crime absorbs another part of this population. Thus the criminal comes in as one of those natural "counterweights" that engender a correct balance and a new list of "useful" occupations.[16]

(5) The effects of the criminal on the development of productive power can be shown in many other aspects. Would locks ever have reached their present degree of excellence had there been no thieves? Would the making of bank-notes have reached its present perfection had there been no forgers? Would the microscope have found its way into the sphere of ordinary commerce (see Babbage) but for trading frauds? Doesn't practical chemistry owe just as much to adulteration of commodities and the efforts to expose it as to the honest zeal for production? Crime, through its constantly new methods of attack on property, constantly calls into being new methods of defense. Internationally, if there were no state crimes, there would be no world markets nor nationalities themselves.[17]

4.4.3 Mid-1870s to Marx's death

The focus of Marx's historical measure changed in his twilight years. He emphasized the value measure for historical progress and severely criticized the heinous crimes of Western colonialists destroying the pre-capitalist social structure without addressing the objective progress capitalism rendered for historical development. For example, in the book *Communal Land Ownership: The Causes, Processes, and Consequences of Its Disintegration*, Kovalevsky pointed out that the British transformed public ownership of land to private ownership of land in the Punjab region of India, drawing on the forests and wastelands of village communes, all of which facilitated the Europeans' colonization of the locals. Excerpting Kovalevsky in *Notes on M. Kovalevsky*, Marx commented: "The English Indian officials and the publicists supported upon these, as Sir H. Maine, etc., describe the decline of common property in the Punjab as the mere result of economic progress," "whereas they themselves are the chief (active)"[18] perpetrators of such decline.

Marx still upheld the following critique of Maine in the first draft of *Marx–Zasulich Correspondence* in 1881:

I shall consider this line of reasoning only in so far as it is based upon European experiences. As regards the East Indies, for example, everyone except Sir H. Maine and his like is aware that the suppression of communal land ownership was nothing but an act of English vandalism which drove the indigenous population backward rather than forward![19]

When Kovalevsky referred to the debate over the plundering of Arab lands by the "French National Assembly" (Marx called it "Assembly of Rurals"), Marx commented: "Hence the first concern of the Assembly of Rurals of 1873 was to hit upon more effective measures for stealing the land of the Arabs." "The debates in this assembly of shame concerning the project 'On the Introduction of Private Property' in Algeria seek to hide the villainy under the so-called eternal, inalterable laws of political economy." "In these debates the 'Rurals' are unanimous on the goal: destruction of collective property. The debate turns only around the method, how to bring it about."

> The British government used "mortgage" and "transfer" (approved by law) to try to disintegrate the collective ownership of the peasants in the northwestern provinces of India and Punjab, completely deprive them, turning the commune land into the private property of the usurers.[20]

In his book *The Aryan Village in India and Ceylon*, Sir John Phear mentioned that *Fixed Arbitrary Weights* introduced in 1793 by the British Indian Governor Cornwallis in Bangladesh made Zamindar, who used to charge the farmers on the land under his jurisdiction on behalf of the British government, become the hereditary owner of the land. "This is the result of a British villain and a donkey,"[21] Marx denounced in *Notes on the Phear's*. In *Ancient Social History Notes* written in his later years, Marx did not talk about the primitive barbarism and backwardness of the former capitalist social structure, nor the Western colonialists' destruction as a historical unconscious tool and their important role in objectively promoting historical progress. A contrast between *Ancient Social History Notes* and the two articles about India written by Marx in 1853 would easily reveal the difference between them and the transformation of Marx's historical evaluation method. What needs to be explained is that although Marx in his later years made the value method or measure the key for historical progress, he did not completely give up the historical measure of historical progress. In his first draft of *Marx–Zasulich Correspondence*, Marx talked about the isolation, originality, and backwardness of the Russian rural commune. He said:

> One debilitating feature of the "agricultural commune" in Russia is inimical to it in every way. This is its isolation, the lack of connection between the lives of different communes. It is not an immanent or universal characteristic of this type that the commune should appear as a localised microcosm. But wherever it does so appear, it leads to the formation of a more or less central despotism above the communes.[22]

Marx believed that in order to make the Russian commune move forward, it was necessary to eliminate the isolation, the primitive nature, and the backwardness of the commune. This represents the historical measure of the Russian society's progress.

Why did Marx change the measuring method of social progress in his later years? This was due to changes in historical conditions which in turn led to different estimates of the revolutionary situation. It was a period of widespread prosperity for Western European capitalism after the failure of the European revolution in 1848 when Marx wrote the two articles about India in 1853. He thought there was no real revolution in the general prosperity. While writing *Ancient Social History Notes* in his later years, Marx realized that these former capitalist social structures were not only phenomena correlated with capitalism, but also representative of "capitalist production engaged in battle in Western Europe as well as the United States," "and it finds it in a crisis which will only end in its elimination, in the return of modern societies to the 'archaic' type of communal property, collective production and procession."[23] Marx always had such an idea that the expansion of Western colonialism in former capitalist countries and regions would lead to the development of capitalism in these countries and regions. Capitalism, though declining in West Europe, was new in the vast land outside West Europe where it newly emerged and developed. Therefore, proletarian revolutions, even if victorious in West Europe, would be localized in scattered pocket areas and would be quickly suppressed in newly capitalistic nations. In the late 1850s, during the capitalist economic crisis in Europe, Marx believed that the storm of revolution would come. In his letter of October 1858 to Engels, he said: "There is no denying that bourgeois society has for the second time experienced its 16th century, a 16th century which, I hope, will sound its death knell just as the first ushered it into the world."

> Since the world is round, the colonization of California and Australia and the opening up of China and Japan would seem to have completed this process. For us, the difficult question is this: on the Continent the revolution is imminent and will, moreover, instantly assume a socialist character. Will it not necessarily be crushed in this little corner of the earth, since the movement of bourgeois society is still in the ascendant over a far greater area?[24]

This thought of Marx remained in his old age. So when he saw capitalism further mired in crisis, he advised the Russians and others in former capitalist countries to "not rush into capitalism,"[25] but to retain the public ownership of land as leverage for social revival, as a starting point for communism. Thus, the transformation of the historical evaluation method of Marx's later years is consistent not only with the objective process of historical development, but also with the internal logic of his own thought development.

Notes

1 *An Anthology of Marx and Engels* (Vol. 8). (2009). Beijing, China: People's Publishing House, 34.
2 *Collected Works of Marx and Engels* (Vol. 2). (1957). Beijing, China: People's Publishing House, 106.
3 *An Anthology of Marx and Engels* (Vol. 4). (2009). Beijing, China: People's Publishing House, 196, 196–197.
4 *An Anthology of Marx and Engels* (Vol. 7). (2009). Beijing, China: People's Publishing House, 928–929.

5 *An Anthology of Marx and Engels* (Vol. 9). (2009). Beijing, China: People's Publishing House, 189.

6 *An Anthology of Marx and Engels* (Vol. 9). (2009). Beijing, China: People's Publishing House, 155–156.

7 *An Anthology of Marx and Engels* (Vol. 9). (2009). Beijing, China: People's Publishing House, 188.

8 *An Anthology of Marx and Engels* (Vol. 2). (2009). Beijing, China: People's Publishing House, 683–682, 686.

9 *An Anthology of Marx and Engels* (Vol. 2). (2009). Beijing, China: People's Publishing House, 690–691.

10 *An Anthology of Marx and Engels* (Vol. 2). (2009). Beijing, China: People's Publishing House, 580.

11 *Collected Works of Marx and Engels* (Vol. 34). (2008). Beijing, China: People's Publishing House, 127–128. Emphasis added.

12 *Collected Works of Marx and Engels* (Vol. 32). (1998). Beijing, China: People's Publishing House, 353.

13 *Collected Works of Marx and Engels* (Vol. 32). (1998). Beijing, China: People's Publishing House, 349.

14 *Collected Works of Marx and Engels* (Vol. 32). (1998). Beijing, China: People's Publishing House, 350.

15 *Collected Works of Marx and Engels* (Vol. 32). (1998). Beijing, China: People's Publishing House, 350.

16 *Collected Works of Marx and Engels* (Vol. 32). (1998). Beijing, China: People's Publishing House, 350.

17 *Collected Works of Marx and Engels* (Vol. 32). (1998). Beijing, China: People's Publishing House, 350–353.

18 Central Compilation and Translation Bureau (Eds. & Trans.). (1996). *Notes on Marx's Ancient Social History*. Beijing, China: People's Publishing House, 94.

19 *An Anthology of Marx and Engels* (Vol. 3). (2009). Beijing, China: People's Publishing House, 581.

20 *Collected Works of Marx and Engels* (Vol. 45). (1985). Beijing, China: People's Publishing House, 322, 324.

21 Central Compilation and Translation Bureau (Eds. & Trans.). (1996). *Notes on Marx's Ancient Social History*. Beijing, China: People's Publishing House, 397.

22 *An Anthology of Marx and Engels* (Vol. 3). (2009). Beijing, China: People's Publishing House, 575.

23 *An Anthology of Marx and Engels* (Vol. 3). (2009). Beijing, China: People's Publishing House, 579.

24 *An Anthology of Marx and Engels* (Vol. 10). (2009). Beijing, China: People's Publishing House, 166.

25 *An Anthology of Marx and Engels* (Vol. 4). (2009). Beijing, China: People's Publishing House, 463.

5   The integrity of Marxism

In his article *Karl Marx*, Lenin believed that Marxism consists of three main components: Marxist philosophy, Marxist political economy, and scientific socialism. These three components, however, are often housed in three different departments in Chinese colleges and universities. As a negative consequence, professors who study and teach one theory are not quite familiar with the other two. The situation has injured the integrity and proper understanding of Marxism. Most Marxist scholars consider Marx's *Capital* not only an economic work, but one of philosophy and scientific socialism that unites various components of Marxism into an organic whole. Since China's reform and opening-up, some scholars in China have conducted interdisciplinary research. For example, many Marxist scholars have researched both the economic and philosophical issues within *Capital* and have produced encouraging results. These results, however, are not always taken up by political economists of Marxism, leading to lack of communication and understanding among scholars studying different components of Marxism. In recent years, different academic departments of Marxist studies have realized the issue and have given attention to the integrity of Marxism. However, textbooks compiled in the field still follow the three separate tracks of Marxist components—a configuration certainly not reflective of the integrity of Marxism.

Marx and Engels' theory on the development trajectory of the oriental society is closely tied to the integrity of Marxism. This theory is neither purely philosophy, nor purely political economics, nor purely scientific socialism, but a synthesis of all three. Only by studying the integrity of Marxism may we derive authentic understandings of Marxism. As illustrated below, controversies, misinterpretations, and distortion of Marxism arise when Marxism is treated not in its integrity.

5.1   The integrity of Marxism from the perspective of its social and historical conditions

Mehring, in his 1893 book *On Historical Materialism*, argued:

> In fact the materialist study of history is of course subject to the very laws of historical motion that it itself lays down. It is the product of historical development; it could not have been imagined in any earlier period by even

the most brilliant mind. The secret of the history of mankind could only be unveiled when a certain historical level had been reached.[1]

Not just historical materialism, but Marxism as a whole, is the product of its historical conditions.

From the 1640s to the mid-1800s, the bourgeois revolutions, successively taking place in major Western European countries such as the United Kingdom and France, overthrew the feudal autocracy, and eliminated the obstacles for and greatly precipitated the capitalist development. The industrial revolution, beginning in England in the 1760s, preluded the capitalist production and the shift from the workshop industry to the machine industry. By the 1830s and 1840s, Britain led the completion of the first industrial revolution through massive mechanization and huge factories. In the same time, the UK became the "world factory" providing the majority of industrial products for the world. The French capitalist economy and industrial revolution, though half a century behind Britain, also developed greatly after its bourgeois revolution in 1789, particularly after the July Revolution in 1830. Lagging behind Britain and France, Germany had only a few factories by the early 19th century. But by the 1830s and 1840s, its capitalist economy garnered rapid development.

The capitalist machine industry greatly boosted productivity, science, and technology, giving unprecedented material growth. However, it also sharpened contradictions within capitalism. One such contradiction is between socialized production and private possession of the means of production. Manifestations of this contradiction were prevalent: Between organized production in individual factories and the anarchy of production in the entire society, between the economy's booming productivity and the working class's dwindling purchasing power. The result was cyclical economic crises that plagued Britain after 1825, all clearly indicating the severity of the contradiction between productivity and the capitalist production relations. However, due to capitalism's internal adjustments, the contradiction was alleviated after late 1800s and particularly after WWII. Nevertheless, it is to stay as long as capitalism still exists.

The intensification of the fundamental contradictions of capitalism was visible foremost in the relation between the working class and the bourgeoisie. By the 1830s and 1840s, major social conflicts in Western Europe shifted from those between the common people and the feudal forces, to those between the working class and the bourgeoisie. Originally the allies of the bourgeoisie in the latter's fight against feudalism, the working class eventually staged their own fight and turned against the bourgeoisie. This fight was triggered by extreme poverty due to capitalist exploitation and oppression. The working class evolved from passive sufferers to revolutionary fighters. They will put capitalism into its grave by erecting a socialist system. As such, the working class was in urgent need of a revolutionary theory to enlighten and guide their historic endeavors. To meet this need, Marx and Engels formulated their theory.

With large-scale socialized production, capitalism showed rapidly changing social relations. People soon learned that no social system is permanent and immutable. A new social form will emerge in lieu of the old to resolve the latter's problems. This is vividly presented in the *Communist Manifesto* by Marx and Engels:

> The bourgeoisie cannot exist without constantly revolutionizing the instruments of production, and thereby the relations of production, and with them the whole relations of society. Conservation of the old modes of production in unaltered form, was, on the contrary, the first condition of existence for all earlier industrial classes. Constant revolutionizing of production, uninterrupted disturbance of all social conditions, everlasting uncertainty and agitation distinguish the bourgeois epoch from all earlier ones. All freed, fast-frozen relations, with their train of ancient and venerable prejudices and opinions, are swept away, all new-formed ones become antiquated before they can ossify. All that is solid melts into air, all that is holy is profaned, and man is at last compelled to face with sober senses, his real conditions of life, and his relations with his kind.[2]

Conclusion can be drawn, from the social-historical conditions in which Marxism was born, that the development of capitalism and the aggravation of its intrinsic problems, along with the fact that the working class stepped onto the historical stage as an independent political force, not only triggered changes in the theories of philosophy, political economics, and socialism, but also helped to integrate these three into a rich Marxist science. Many factors help in the revelation of laws of nature, society, and human thinking, and the founding of a philosophy about the world and its history, including the production mode of capitalism with its internal contradictions, the development of productivity and scientific technologies, and recurrent social disturbance and changes. Meanwhile, the production mode of capitalism and the development of its intrinsic contradictions revealed the nature of the capitalist mode of production and facilitated the discovery of the theory of surplus value. Based on the scientific conceptions of the world and history, and the theory of surplus value, Marx and Engels solved the theoretical problems that were left unsolved by utopian socialists. Marxist theories turned socialism from a utopian dream into a scientific system. Marxism offers a comprehensive anatomy of the capitalist production mode, the class structure in a capitalist society, and the working class' misery and mission. Therefore, Marxism, as a science that aims to free the working class and humanity, was a unified system of philosophy, political economics, and scientific socialism.

5.2 The integrity of Marxism based on the origins of Marxism

The historical times of Marx and Engels and the tasks of those times provided the objective conditions for the birth of Marxism, but these conditions would not automatically give birth to a theory. Any new theory or doctrine starts from and as a critical inheritance of its predecessors. As pointed out by Marx, "The philosophy of any age as a discipline of its own is bequeathed by its predecessors, which provide the cognitive materials for the former."[3] This is true for philosophy, as for political economics and socialism. The theoretical origins of Marxism include the classical German philosophy, the classical British political economics, and the utopian socialism of the UK and France in the early 1800s. These origins together represented the pinnacle of human ideology at their time and will receive a synopsis below.

First, we will discuss the classical German philosophy. This philosophy is of the century between the mid-1700s and the mid-1800s, when the bourgeoisie was emerging, growing, and preparing for the bourgeois revolution. It includes the philosophy of Kant, Fichte, Schelling, Hegel, and Feuerbach. The highest achievements of the classical German philosophy are the dialectical method of Hegel and materialism of Feuerbach. Hegel is the first philosopher in the history of philosophy who, in the form of idealism, has systematically explained the basic laws of the dialectical method, including the law of unity of opposites, the law of exchange between quality and quantity, and the law of the negation of negation. By applying the dialectical method to the study of human history, Hegel depicted the history of human society as an inevitable progressive process independent of human will. However, the dialectical method of Hegel and his conception of history were characterized by occultism and failed to comprehensively incorporate actual historical development. Marx and Engels imbibed the strengths of the dialectical method and its conception of history while criticizing its idealism and occultism. Marx and Engels' revised version of Hegel is known as materialistic dialectics and historical materialism.

Feuerbach, the last representative of classical German philosophy, is an intermediary between Hegel's and Marx's philosophy. As his greatest achievement, Feuerbach restored the authority of materialism through trenchant criticism of theology and idealism. But just as every old school of materialism has its flaws, the materialism of Feuerbach was mechanical and metaphysical, as seen in its treatment of history. Marx and Engels never completely endorsed Feuerbach. Instead, they took in the fundamentals of his materialism but abandoned his abstract humanism and naturalism, thus cleansing Feuerbach of the metaphysical and idealistic impurities.

More broadly, Marxist philosophy originates not just from classical German philosophy. Many other philosophical achievements nourished Marxist philosophy. Ancient Greek-Roman philosophy, of which Marx and Engels conducted a profound study, cannot be excluded. Moreover, Marx and Engels had studied modern European philosophy, especially British philosophy represented by Francis Bacon, Thomas Hobbes, John Locke, George Berkeley, and David Hume. Marx and Engels also studied French encyclopedic philosophers represented by La Mettrie, Helvetius, Denis Diderot, and Holbach. Therefore, neither modern British philosophy nor modern French philosophy should be excluded from the origins of Marxist philosophy. In conclusion, the theoretical origins of Marxism include the fruits of all pre-Marxist European philosophies, of which classical German philosophy rendered a direct influence while others an indirect one.

Two "separations" existed in pre-Marxist philosophies. The first is between materialism and dialectics, evidenced by Hegel's dialectics divorced of materialism. The second separation is between the materialistic conception of nature and the materialistic conception of history, evidenced by the fact that Feuerbach was materialistic about nature but idealistic about history. Marxism, by bridging these two separations, achieved unity between materialism and dialectics, between the materialistic conception of nature and the materialistic conception of history. Consequently, Marxist philosophy represents a complete materialism that encompasses both nature and history.

Second, we will explore the classical British political economics. The classical British political economics represented the interests of the emerging bourgeoisie when the bourgeois production mode had been established and yet the conflict between the proletariat and the bourgeoisie was just budding. This school of economics started in the second half of the 17th century (the time of the British bourgeois revolution) and matured in the early 19th century. It was founded by William Petty, developed by Adam Smith, and ended with David Ricardo. Classical political economics was a vital theoretical weapon for the emerging bourgeoisie's fight against the backward feudalism, and established and solidified the capitalist production mode. Marx said,

> The Classics, like Adam Smith and Ricardo, represent a bourgeoisie which, while still struggling with the relics of feudal society, works only to purge economic relations of feudal taints, to increase the productive forces and to give a new upsurge to industry and commerce.[4]

The classical political economists had put forward many valuable economic theories, such as labor being the only source of value, the general abstraction of labor, the classification of value into use value and exchange value, the origin of surplus value in the analysis of salary, profit, and land rent, and the economic analysis of class relations in capitalist society. All these played a positive role in the emergence of the political economics of Marxism. Limited by time and class perspective, the classical political economics suffered serious flaws. For instance, it saw capitalism as compatible with human nature and thus permanently immutable; it is idealistic and metaphysical about capitalism; and it is contradictory and chaotic in its theory of value. Marx and Engels critically incorporated the fruits of classical political economics, tapped a massive quantity of historical materials regarding capitalism, and illuminated the economic structures of capitalism and its inherent contradictions. As a result, the theory of Marx and Engels is able to elucidate the nature of the capitalistic production mode and the course of its emergence, development, and demise. Most importantly, Marx and Engels revolutionized political economics through the rigorous concepts of labor value and surplus value—the latter a derivative from labor value.

Finally, we will explore British and French utopian socialism. This refers to theories of three utopian socialists—Saint-Simon, Fourier, and Robert Owen—founded in the first half of the 19th century. The classical German philosophy and the classical British political economics, in their class attributes and social functions, defended the interests of the bourgeoisie and its capitalist system. Utopian socialism, however, vigorously attacked the bourgeoisie's capitalism. For instance, Saint-Simon saw capitalism as "a new form of slavery"; Fourier called it "social hell" and "revived slavery"; Owen deemed it "a full system of deception and hypocrisy" corrupted by the evil trinity of private ownership, religion, and its marriage paradigm. Unlike the British classical political economists who saw capitalism as the eternal and final social system, utopian socialists considered it nothing but a phase of social development. They envisioned that a better future society will replace capitalism. Saint-Simon called his envisioned society the "industrial system," where people would use science, art, and technology to meet people's needs. Fourier named his ideal society the "harmonious institution," where people live in harmony and all members' desires would be fully fulfilled. Owen's vision was even more radical than those of Saint-Simon and Fourier, who still endorsed private ownership. Owen wanted a united community of communists based on shared ownership and the abolition of the state. Utopian socialists' visions of future societies had reasonable elements, such as the elimination of the old labor division, of differences between urban and rural areas, between industrial enterprises and agriculture, and between mental and manual labor; early integration of education and production labor; the shift from management of people to that of materials and production; and abolition of the state. These thoughts provided the ideological foundations for our vision of the future society. Nevertheless, the theories of our three utopian socialists, limited by their historical times, suffered several flaws. They believed that human reason can supersede the objective world. They denied class struggles and the necessity of violent revolution. In short, they were too idealistic. Furthermore, their over-explicit depiction of future society with all its ideal details was largely fantasy. They failed to recognize the revolutionary power and historical mission of the proletariat and could not find the social power to realize their concepts of future society. Based on a materialistic conception of history and their theory of surplus value, Marx and Engels insightfully studied capitalism's intrinsic contradiction and development trajectory, synthesized the working class's experience in class struggle, critically imbibed the fruits of utopian socialism, envisioned the characteristics of socialism and communism in the future, and revolutionized the socialist theory via scientific socialism.

By now, we have explained the influence of the classical German philosophy upon Marxist philosophy, the influence of the classical British political economics upon Marxist political economics, and the influence of the utopian socialism upon Marxist scientific socialism. Since these three influences were largely of the same historical time, they are not independent from and mutually exclusive of each other, but interconnected with and mutually influential upon each other. The same applies to their aggregated influences upon the philosophy of Marx and Engels. Specifically, Marxist political economics saw its origins in British classical political economics, its methodology in classical German dialectics, and its direction and goals in utopian socialism. Similar influences apply to Marxist socialist theories. Hence, based on its theoretical origins, Marxism is an integrated system comprising Marxist philosophy, Marxist political economics, and Marxist scientific socialism.

In addition to the above three direct theoretical influences, the birth of Marxism also benefited from the great progress of natural science at its time. Thanks to the capitalist mode of production, modern natural science, liberated from the shackles of medieval theology, flourished. After the mid-18th century, especially in the early 19th century, modern natural science developed from "the science of gathering materials" (i.e., "the science about existing things") to "the science of organizing materials" (i.e., "the science about the occurrence and development of things and their interconnections").[5] During this period, a series of new disciplines emerged, such as geology, embryology, animal and plant physiology, and organic chemistry. In particular, the three major discoveries of the natural science—cytology, biological evolution, and the law of energy conversion and conservation—exerted an enormous impact on Marxism. Plants and animals are the result of the growth of cells in accordance with natural laws, elucidating the internal unity among living organisms. This view radically shook the theological outlook of "God created everything" and the metaphysical concept of the invariance of species. The law of energy conversion and conservation reveals the role of various forms of energy in nature, such as mechanical energy, thermal energy, optical energy, electromagnetic energy, and chemical energy, all of which result from various motions of matter. As they interact with each other according to certain metrics, the total amount of energy in the conversion process stays the same. It proves that material motion is objective, and can be neither created nor destroyed, but only transformed from one form to another. And the various forms of motion of the material are internally unified. Biological evolutionism reveals that the various organisms existing today, including human beings, are evolved from primitive single-cell embryos according to the rules of "survival competition," "natural selection," and "survival of the fittest." Since then, the concept of change and development was introduced into the biological world. In short, the development of natural sciences laid a theoretical foundation for Marxist philosophy. Natural sciences represent an intellectual form of productive forces.

These productive forces generate material wealth and constitute the scientific premise of the industrial revolution. They transformed handicraft workshops into large-scale machinery industry. The development of natural sciences directly or indirectly affected the social structure of the capitalist society, the relations of production, and the growth of the ideological awareness of the proletariat. It laid the scientific foundation for Marxist philosophy, Marxist political economics, and Marx's theory of scientific socialism. The influences from the natural sciences again demonstrate the integrity of Marxism.

5.3 Integrity of Marxism as based on its content

Marxist philosophy, political economics, and scientific socialism are not isolated from or irrelevant to each other. Instead, they together constitute a scientific system with inherent logical connections. In the entire Marxist theoretical system, philosophy is the guiding principle of its world outlook and methodology; the political economics is the analysis of the capitalist mode of production guided by the philosophical worldview and methodology; the scientific socialism is the result of using philosophy to analyze economic facts. The three parts infiltrate and complement each other to form a unified system of Marxism.

First, under the guidance of materialistic dialectics, Marxist political economics uses basic historical materialism to analyze the capitalist mode of production, thereby overcoming the shortcomings of classical British economics and making revolutionizing changes in the field of political economics. Marxist political economics highlights the brilliant elements of materialistic dialectics and historical materialism. In the meantime, it has enriched and developed the basic concepts and principles of the materialistic dialectics. It has theoretically demonstrated and enriched the science of historical materialism.

Second, scientific socialism cannot emerge without the guidance of Marxist philosophy. Engels made a profound argument on this issue in 1882 in the preface to the first German edition of *Socialism: Utopian and Scientific*. He said,

> But scientific socialism is after all an essentially German product and could arise only in that nation whose classical philosophy had kept alive the tradition of conscious dialectics: in Germany. The materialistic conception of history and its specific application to the modern class struggle between proletariat and bourgeoisie was only possible by means of dialectics.[6]

Third, viewed from the relationship between political economics and scientific socialism, Marxist political economics created the theory of surplus value via scientifically analyzing the capitalist mode of production. It reveals the basic contradiction and development law of capitalism, and demonstrates the inevitability of capitalism's demise and socialism's victory; it illustrates the class status and historical mission of the proletariat, and makes the scientific projections and assumptions for the characteristics of future socialist and communist societies; moreover, it indicates the trajectory for the proletariat to overthrow capitalism and construct socialism. Without a science of the laws for the capitalist economy, there won't be a scientific socialist theory. Therefore, Engels said in *Anti-Dühring*, "With these two great discoveries, the materialistic conception of history and the revelation of the secret of capitalistic production through surplus-value ... socialism became a science."[7]

Finally, many concepts and principles are shared by the three major components of Marxism, such as (1) productive forces, production relations, and production modes—the production relations must be adapted to the nature of productive forces; (2) economic foundation and the superstructure—the latter must be suited to the former; (3) class, state, revolution, and reform—the role of class struggle in social development and the role of revolution and reforms in social development; (4) society, social structure, and social formations—the alternation of social formations and the development of social formations are natural historical processes; (5) capitalism, socialism, and communism—the transition from capitalism to socialism and the basic characteristics thereof; (6) the basic characteristics of the socialist society and the communist society; (7) socialism in its due course develops into communism; and (8) the freedom and liberation of human beings, the union of free individuals, and a leap from the realm of necessity to the realm of freedom, etc.

5.4 The integrity of Marxism based on its historical evolution

Marxism was established in the mid-1840s and has a history of 170 years. Ever since its establishment, during the process of answering important theoretical questions presented by the practice of different historical periods, Marxism has continuously enriched and developed itself, producing a vibrant stream of ideas of unceasing innovation and vitality, and successive adjustments entailed by historical developments.

Marx and Engels are both founders and developers of Marxism. The *Theses on Feuerbach* written by Marx in the spring of 1845 and *The German Ideology* written by Marx and Engels during 1945 and 1946 inaugurated basic Marxism. *The Poverty of Philosophy* by Marx published in July 1847 and *The Communist Manifesto* by Marx and Engels published in February 1848 marked the official publication of Marxism. Shortly after its birth, Marxism underwent its baptism in the European Revolutions in 1848, and later stood the test of the Paris Commune in 1871, through which it further developed. In this process, Marx and Engels continued to advance their theory, by synthesizing practical experience and theoretical researches, as well as by defending it against opponents. In its introduction, Marxism had not yet completed its political-economic critique, which did not occur until decades of hard work with the publication of Marx's masterpiece *Capital*. In the 1870s and 1880s, Engels systematically studied the philosophical issues in nature and natural science, and wrote *Natural Dialectics*, which initiated a new field of Marxism on nature. After the mid-1870s, Engels finished *Anti-Dühring* and *Ludwig Feuerbach and the End of Classical German Philosophy* and other works, which comprehensively and systematically expounded every component of Marxism. The writings of Marx and Engels on the development trajectory of Russian society in their later years greatly enriched and developed Marxism. *Notes of the Ancient Social History* and *Notes of History* written by Marx in his later years, along with *The Origin of the Family, Private Property and the State* written by Engels, based on Marx's above *Notes* and other new materials about ancient history, studied pre-capitalist social formations, and comprehensively discussed the entire process and development laws of human history. A series of letters written by Engels in the 1880s and 1890s and prefaces and introductions to Marx and Engels' previous works further developed Marxism. At the turn of the 20th century, some Marxists in Europe, such as Mehring, Kautsky, Rosa Luxemburg, Lafargue, Labriola, and Plekhanov, also contributed to the development of Marxism at different levels.

After the death of Marx and Engels, against the backdrop of imperialism and the proletarian revolution, during his leadership of Russia's proletarian revolution and socialist construction and his fights against opportunism in the Second International, Lenin inherited, defended, and developed Marxism, and advanced it into the new stage of Leninism. Lenin defended and advanced Marxist philosophy in his books such as *Materialism and Empirio-Criticism* and *Philosophical Notes*; defended and developed Marxist political economics in his books such as *The Development of Capitalism in Russia* and *Imperialism, the Highest Stage of Capitalism*; and defended and developed the theory of scientific socialism in works such as *The State and Revolution, Left-Wing Communism: An Infantile Disorder, On the Revolution of Our Country*, and *On Cooperative*. Particularly, Lenin's two papers, *On the Slogan of Federal Europe* and *The Military Programme of the Proletarian Revolution*, suggest that the socialist revolution, under certain historical conditions, may witness victory in one or several countries first. Before the October Revolution and after its victory, he on several occasions said that backward countries could transform from capitalism into socialism, and presented his thoughts, among others, of the "new economic policy." Lenin's thoughts provided significant guidance for socialist revolution and construction in backward countries.

Marxism was introduced to China between the 19th and 20th centuries. In the process of guiding China's revolution and construction, a Sinicized Marxism has been formed, namely Marxism with Chinese Characteristics (aka Marxism with Chinese style or Marxism in Chinese manner). The history of Marxism in China is a history of combining the basic principles of Marxism with the reality of China. During the new-democratic revolution, the Chinese communists, represented by Mao Zedong, found a revolutionary path fit to China's realities, creatively developed Marxism, and built Mao Zedong Thought, by summing up previous successful and unsuccessful experiences while carrying out their own explorations. Since the founding of New China, the leading group represented by Mao Zedong carried out numerous explorations of China's socialist transformation and the road to socialist construction, through which some original theoretical achievements and other great achievements were realized, thus providing valuable experience, theoretical preparation, and material foundation for the building of socialism with Chinese characteristics in a new historical period. Since China's reform and opening-up, the Chinese Communist Party has blazed a new path of socialism with Chinese characteristics. China's socialist theory comprises Deng Xiaoping Theory, the important thoughts of "Three Representations," and the scientific outlook on development. This theoretical system adheres to and develops Marxism-Leninism and Mao Zedong Thought. It integrates the wisdom garnered during China's socialist construction. It is the latest achievement of the localization of Marxism in China, the most valuable political and spiritual wealth of the Party, and the common ideological foundation for the people of all ethnic groups of China to jointly make promising efforts. In contemporary China, sticking to the theoretical system of socialism with Chinese characteristics is to truly uphold Marxism. Since the 18th CPC National Congress, General Secretary Xi Jinping has delivered a series of important speeches, offering a series of answers to guide the development of the Party and the country. These speeches involve reform, development, stability, internal affairs, diplomacy, national defense, and various aspects of governing the Party, the country, and the army. They provide the action plan for our Party to govern the country under new historical conditions; they are the latest results of adhering to and developing socialism with Chinese character- istics; they provide the necessary ideological weapons for Chinese people to win the socialist war with Chinese characteristics, and achieve the Chinese Dream of rejuvenating a new China.

The development of Marxism was a tortuous process—continuous but with twists and turns. During its growth, Marxism has been resisted or distorted by old forces and ideas, and suffered setbacks, albeit temporarily, during the low tide of the socialist movement. Moreover, some incorrect opinions were put forward due to mistakes in practice and understanding. To study the history of Marxism, we need to investigate both its general trend, its mistakes, twists and turns, tem- porary regressions, and the causes thereof. Thus, we can learn lessons, overcome and eliminate inaccurate viewpoints, and promote the healthy furtherance of Marxism. Looking through the 170-year-long history of Marxism, we can clearly see that Marxism boasts as being a holistic scientific theory founded and devel- oped by its founders Marx and Engels and such successors as Lenin, Mao Zedong, and Deng Xiaoping. If any of its components were removed, Marxism would be fragmentary and incomplete. As based on its development history, the integrity of Marxism needs to be viewed as a dynamic process.

5.5 Viewing the integrity of Marxism from Marxist classics

Most Marxist classics encompass philosophy, political economics, and scientific socialism. Despite the specialty of each discipline, its central questions incorpo- rate all three areas.

Marx's *Economics & Philosophy Manuscripts of 1844* is such a work. So are some inaugural works of Marxism, including *The German Ideology*, *The Poverty of Philosophy*, and *Manifesto of the Communist Party*. All these works not only comprehensively discuss philosophy, political economics, and scientific social- ism, but also clarify the strategies and tactics of the class struggle of the proletariat.

Marx's *Capital* is a work on economics, philosophy, and scientific social- ism. In its elaboration of political economics, *Capital* has presented insights on numerous philosophical issues: The dialectical implications in the duality of com- modities and labor; fetishism of commodity, capital, and interest in the economic- philosophical discussion of commodity, capital, and interest; and revelations about social development in its discussion of average profit rate. "Under capitalist production, the general law acts as the prevailing tendency only in a very compli- cated and approximate manner, as a never ascertainable average of ceaseless fluc- tuations."[8] When discussing the tendency of the profit rate, Engels said, "None of [the profit] has any reality except as approximation, tendency, average, and not as immediate reality."[9] The discussion in *Capital* of the capitalist production mode reveals that socialism will eventually replace capitalism. Different components of Marxism are highly integrated in *Capital*. Engels' *Anti-Dühring* addresses (the interconnections of) the three major parts of Marxism: philosophy, socialism, and political economics. Discussion of these three parts are seen also in Lenin's works such as *What the "Friends of the People" Are and How They Fight the Social-Democrats*; *Materialism and Empirio-Criticism*; *Imperialism, the Highest Stage of Capitalism*; and *The State and Revolution*. Mao Zedong's *Analysis of Chinese Classes*, *Strategies for Chinese Revolutionary War*, *On Protracted War*, *On New Democracy*, and *Correctly Handling Contradictions among the People* also embed the three components of Marxism. Recent and contemporary Chinese leaders Deng Xiaoping, Jiang Zemin, Hu Jintao, and Xi Jinping have extended the Marxist discussion of socialism. The interconnections of the major components of Marxism are seen in the works of Marx and Engels and their disciples.

As such, the three parts—Marxist philosophy, Marxist political economics, and scientific socialism—need to be treated as an organic unity. In the past decade or so, China has set up the first-level discipline of Marxist studies and compiled necessary teaching materials. One of its valuable goals is to study and understand Marxism as an organic whole and implement this approach in our teaching practice. The actual practice of our teaching, however, falls short of the purported goal. The three components of Marxism are still presented as three disparate dishes on our platter of education. We must cultivate a new crop of teacher to execute the job effectively, which perhaps should proceed even before the creation of necessary additional teaching materials. My recent efforts in advocating the integrity of Marxism include dozens of academic papers produced on the basis of *Capital* and its manuscripts. However, my work has not matured to a degree to render a comprehensive textbook, for the fruition of which I invite efforts from my peers.

Notes

1   Mehring, F. (1981). *Defend Marxism* (Ji Hong, Trans.). Beijing, China: People's Publishing House. 3.

2   *An Anthology of Marx and Engels* (Vol. 2). (2009). Beijing, China: People's Publishing House, 34–35.

3   *An Anthology of Marx and Engels* (Vol. 10). (2009). Beijing, China: People's Publishing House, 599.

4   *An Anthology of Marx and Engels* (Vol. 1). (2009). Beijing, China: People's Publishing House, 615.

5   *An Anthology of Marx and Engels* (Vol. 4). (2009). Beijing, China: People's Publishing House, 299–300.

6   *An Anthology of Marx and Engels* (Vol. 3). (2009). Beijing, China: People's Publishing House, 495–496.

7   *An Anthology of Marx and Engels* (Vol. 9). (2009). Beijing, China: People's Publishing House, 30.

8   *An Anthology of Marx and Engels* (Vol. 5). (2009). Beijing, China: People's Publishing House, 181.

9   *An Anthology of Marx and Engels* (Vol. 5). (2009). Beijing, China: People's Publishing House, 693–694.

Bibliography

Classic works of Marxism

An Anthology of Mao Zedong (Vol. 8). (1999). Beijing, China: People's Publishing House.

An Anthology of Marx and Engels (Vols. 1–10). (2009). Beijing, China: People's Publishing House.

Collected Works of Lenin (Vol. 1). (1984). Beijing, China: People's Publishing House.

Collected Works of Lenin (Vol. 10). (1987). Beijing, China: People's Publishing House.

Collected Works of Lenin (Vol. 11). (1987). Beijing, China: People's Publishing House.

Collected Works of Lenin (Vol. 12). (1987). Beijing, China: People's Publishing House.

Collected Works of Lenin (Vol. 32). (1985). Beijing, China: People's Publishing House.

Collected Works of Lenin (Vol. 33). (1985). Beijing, China: People's Publishing House.

Collected Works of Lenin (Vol. 34). (1985). Beijing, China: People's Publishing House.

Collected Works of Lenin (Vol. 35). (1985). Beijing, China: People's Publishing House.

Collected Works of Lenin (Vol. 36). (1985). Beijing, China: People's Publishing House.

Collected Works of Lenin (Vol. 37). (1986). Beijing, China: People's Publishing House.

Collected Works of Lenin (Vol. 38). (1986). Beijing, China: People's Publishing House.

Collected Works of Lenin (Vol. 40). (1986). Beijing, China: People's Publishing House.

Collected Works of Lenin (Vol. 41). (1986). Beijing, China: People's Publishing House.

Collected Works of Lenin (Vol. 42). (1987). Beijing, China: People's Publishing House.

Collected Works of Lenin (Vol. 43). (1987). Beijing, China: People's Publishing House.

Collected Works of Lenin (Vol. 55). (1990). Beijing, China: People's Publishing House.

Collected Works of Marx and Engels (Vol. 1). (1955). Beijing, China: People's Publishing House.

Collected Works of Marx and Engels (Vol. 3). (1960). Beijing, China: People's Publishing House.

Collected Works of Marx and Engels (Vol. 19). (1963). Beijing, China: People's Publishing House.

Collected Works of Marx and Engels (Vol. 20). (1971). Beijing, China: People's Publishing House.

Collected Works of Marx and Engels (Vol. 28). (1973). Beijing, China: People's Publishing House.

Collected Works of Marx and Engels (Vol. 32). (1974). Beijing, China: People's Publishing House.

Collected Works of Marx and Engels (Vol. 33). (1973). Beijing, China: People's Publishing House.

Collected Works of Marx and Engels (Vol. 35). (1971). Beijing, China: People's Publishing House.

Collected Works of Marx and Engels (Vol. 39). (1974). Beijing, China: People's Publishing House.

Collected Works of Marx and Engels (Vol. 1). (1995). Beijing, China: People's Publishing House.

Collected Works of Marx and Engels (Vol. 3). (2002). Beijing, China: People's Publishing House.

Collected Works of Marx and Engels (Vol. 21). (2003). Beijing, China: People's Publishing House.

Collected Works of Marx and Engels (Vol. 30). (1995). Beijing, China: People's Publishing House.

Collected Works of Marx and Engels (Vol. 31). (1998). Beijing, China: People's Publishing House.

Collected Works of Marx and Engels (Vol. 32). (1998). Beijing, China: People's Publishing House.

Collected Works of Marx and Engels (Vol. 33). (2004). Beijing, China: People's Publishing House.

Collected Works of Marx and Engels (Vol. 34). (2008). Beijing, China: People's Publishing House.

Selected Readings From the Works of Mao Zedong (Vols. 1–2). (1986). Beijing, China: People's Publishing House.

Selected Works of Lenin (Vols. 1–4). (1995). Beijing, China: People's Publishing House.

Selected Works of Mao Zedong (Vols. 1–4). (1991). Beijing, China: People's Publishing House.

Selected Works of Marx and Engels (Vols. 1–4). (1995). Beijing, China: People's Publishing House.

Chinese literature

Editing Group of *Guide to the Reading of Philosophical Classical Works of Marx, Engels, and Lenin* (Eds.). (2012). *Guide to the Reading of Philosophical Classical Works of Marx, Engels, and Lenin*. Beijing, China: People's Publishing House and Higher Education Press.

Editing Group of *The History of Marxist Philosophy* (Eds.). (2012). *The History of Marxist Philosophy*. Beijing, China: People's Publishing House and Higher Education Press.

Editing Group of *Introduction to Scientific Socialism* (Eds.). (2011). *Introduction to Scientific Socialism*. Beijing, China: People's Publishing House and Higher Education Press.

Fulin, Zhuang. (1996). *The History of Marxism* (Vols. 1–4). Beijing, China: People's Publishing House.

Nansen, Huang et al. (1996). *History of Marxist Philosophy* (Vol. 3). Beijing, China: Beijing Publishing House.

Qiliang, Liu. (1994). *Marx's Theory of the Oriental Society*. Shanghai, China: Xuelin Press.

Xianda, Chen. (1987). *To the Depths of History—A Study of Marx's View of History*. Shanghai, China: Shanghai People's Publishing House.

Yanqing, Chen et al. (1996). *The Introduction to Modern Materialism*. Tianjin, China: Nankai University Press.

Yue, Lu et al. (1992). *The Creative Exploration of Marx in His Later Years—On "Anthropological Notes"*. Zhengzhou, China: Henan People's Publishing House.

Other literature: translations

Bentley, J., & Ziegler, H. (2007). *Traditions & Encounters* (Vols. 1–2) (3rd ed.) (Wei Fenglian et al., Trans.). Beijing, China: Peking University Press.

Hegel, G. W. F. (1956). *Historical Philosophy* (Wang Zaoshi, Trans.). Shanghai, China: SDX Joint Publishing Company.

Hegel, G. W. F. (1980). *The Shorter Logic* (He Lin, Trans.). Beijing, China: The Commercial Press.

Melotti, U. (1981). *Marx and the Third World* (Gao Xian et al., Trans.). Beijing, China: The Commercial Press.

Montesquieu, C. (1961). *The Spirit of the Laws* (Vols. 1–2) (Zhang Yanshen, Trans.). Beijing, China: The Commercial Press.

Rousseau, J. J. (2009). *On the Origin of Human Inequality* (Lü Zhuo, Trans.). Beijing, China: China Social Sciences Press.

Rousseau, J. J. (2009). *The Social Contract* (Xu Qiang, Trans.). Beijing, China: China Social Sciences Press.

Smith, A. (1997). *The Theory of Moral Sentiments* (Jiang Ziqiang et al., Trans.). Beijing, China: The Commercial Press.

Smith, A. (2001). *An Inquiry into the Nature and Causes of the Wealth of Nations* (Yang Jingnian, Trans.). Xi'an, China: Shaanxi People's Publishing House.

Spengler, O. (1963). *The Decline of the West* (Vols. 1–2) (Qi Shirong et al., Trans.). Beijing, China: The Commercial Press.

Toynbee, A. (1964). *A Study of History* (Vols. 1–3) (Cao Mofeng et al., Trans.). Shanghai, China: Shanghai People's Publishing House.

Vico, G. (1989). *New Science* (Zhu Guangqian, Trans.). Beijing, China: The Commercial Press.

Index